Best Easy Day Hikes Series

Best Easy Day Hikes
San Francisco
Peninsula

Tracy Salcedo-Chourré

FALCONGUIDES ®

GUILFORD, CONNECTICUT
HELENA, MONTANA

AN IMPRINT OF THE GLOBE PEQUOT PRESS

Copyright © 2009 by Morris Book Publishing, LLC

Maps by DesignMaps © Morris Book
Publishing, LLC

Library of Congress Cataloging-in-
Publication Data is available on file.

ISBN 978-0-7627-5114-3

Printed in the United States of America

10 9 8 7 6 5 4 3 2 1

Contents

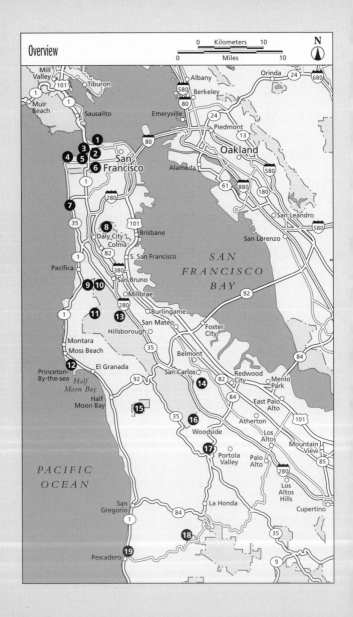

0   Kilometers   10

0   Miles   10

N

Mill Valley

Tiburon

Muir Beach

Sausalito

Albany

Orinda

Berkeley

Emeryville

Piedmont

Oakland

Alameda

San Francisco

San Leandro

San Lorenzo

SAN FRANCISCO BAY

Brisbane

Daly City

Colma

S. San Francisco

Pacifica

San Bruno

Millbrae

Burlingame

San Mateo

Foster City

Hillsborough

Montara

Moss Beach

Belmont

San Carlos

Redwood City

Menlo Park

Princeton-By-the-sea

El Granada

Half Moon Bay

Half Moon Bay

East Palo Alto

Atherton

Woodside

Los Altos

Mountain View

Portola Valley

Palo Alto

Los Altos Hills

Cupertino

PACIFIC OCEAN

San Gregorio

La Honda

Pescadero

Acknowledgments

I am indebted to the many hikers and lovers of wildlands who have worked over the years to preserve parks and trails throughout the Bay Area. A guidebook like this wouldn't be possible without their efforts.

Thanks to the land managers who have taken the time to review the hikes described in this guide, and to guide-book authors who have shared their impressions of and experiences on San Francisco–area trails both in books and online.

In particular I'd like to thank Brenda Bennett and Super-intendent Dave Moore of the San Mateo County Depart-ment of Parks, Chris Detwiller of the Peninsula Open Space Trust, and Nelle Lyons of California State Parks for their input on hike descriptions.

Thanks to The Globe Pequot Press and its fine editors and production staff for inviting me to take on this project and helping me make it the best it can be.

Thanks also to family, friends, and neighbors who either introduced me to trails on the San Francisco Peninsula over the years or offered suggestions for this guide, including Mike Witkowski, the Chourré clan, Jesse and Judy Salcedo, Nick and Nancy Salcedo, Chris Salcedo and Angela Jones, and others.

My husband, Martin, and sons, Jesse, Cruz, and Penn, are all great hikers and unfailing supporters of my work as a writer and teacher. I'm forever grateful to them.

Introduction

It never fails. Screaming into the Waldo Tunnel at 60 miles per hour, I can feel the excitement gather in my belly. Out the other end and there it is: the Golden Gate Bridge. Brick-red towers catching the sun or disappearing into the fog, streams of people flowing by on its walkways, the land disappearing into the deep strait below. I am thrilled. It's simply spectacular.

My love affair with the San Francisco Bay Area, and its signature landmark, has never lost its intensity. Seven generations of family on my mother's side have called the city home, so it may be in my blood. I was born here, grew up in the city's suburbs, and after a long sojourn in the mountains of Colorado, came back to raise my own family in the North Bay.

Like many, I've been nurtured by the Bay Area's fine restaurants, music, museums, universities, theaters, and free-thinking population. But most profoundly, I've been shaped by its natural beauty. The contours of dunes, the play of surf on sand, the moistness of redwood groves, the smell of bay laurel on a hot summer afternoon, waves of golden grasses and bright fields of lupines and poppies stretched over rolling hills . . . It's no wonder that one day I'd write a guide that would lead others into the hills and along the beaches and bluffs.

In the course of researching this book, I've revisited trails I've hiked before and discovered some that are new to me. Each recommends itself in a unique fashion, whether for its ecology, history, or topography. From the Pescadero Marsh to the top of San Bruno Mountain, I am confident that you'll find these hikes as eye opening and satisfying as I have.

The Nature of the Bay

San Francisco and the peninsula are benevolent to trail wanderers. The population is almost universally outdoorsy, with interests ranging from the easy, such as gardening in boxes outside their apartment windows, to the extreme, such as hang gliding and triathlons that include swimming from Alcatraz Island across the bay to the city.

Hiking strikes a middle ground, and this guide seeks to strike a middle ground as well, showcasing relatively short routes that will take trekkers into just about every habitat the Bay Area encompasses. Here you'll find hikes that meander through redwood groves; oceanside marshes, beaches, and blufftops; coastal mountaintops and ridges; oak woodlands; and along the San Andreas Fault rift zone.

Weather

You've probably heard the joke about how the coldest winter you'll ever spend is a summer in San Francisco. While you can pretty much bet on a cold, damp fog bank burying the city on summer days, it never gets so cold that your nose hairs freeze stiff. Throw on the appropriate layers of clothing, and you can venture onto most trails even on the foggiest days.

The San Francisco Bay Area essentially has two seasons: dry and rainy. In the rainy season, which generally runs November through March, temperatures are cool but moderate, ranging from nighttime lows in the 30s and 40s to daytime highs in the 50s and 60s. There can be cold spells, when the temperature drops below freezing, but these are almost as rare as snow on the Golden Gate Bridge . . . once in a hundred years, they say.

In the dry season, April through October, coast-side temperatures seldom exceed the 80s and generally hover in the 60s and 70s. Temperatures inland are higher, ranging from the 70s to the 80s, with the occasional heat wave shooting the mercury above 100 degrees. These are generally short-lived, as the bay's natural air conditioner—the fog—inevitably creeps back in.

Critters

Most likely you'll encounter only benign, sweet creatures on these trails, such as deer, squirrels, rabbits, and a variety of songbirds and shorebirds.

But some of the San Francisco Peninsula's wildlands are habitat for mountain lions and rattlesnakes. Trail managers post signs at trailheads warning hikers if these animals might be present. Encounters are infrequent, but you should familiarize yourself with the proper behavior should you run across either a dangerous snake or cat. Snakes generally strike only if they are threatened. Keep your distance, and they will keep theirs. If you come across a cat, make yourself as big as possible and do *not* run. If you don't act or look like prey, you stand a good chance of not being attacked.

Be Prepared

It would be tough to find a safer place for a hike than on the San Francisco Peninsula. Still, hikers should be prepared, whether they are out for a short stroll on the Golden Gate Promenade or headed deep into the coastal mountains.

Some specific advice:

- Know the basics of first aid, including how to treat bleeding; bites and stings; and fractures, strains, or sprains. Pack a first-aid kit on each excursion.
- Be prepared for both heat and cold by dressing in layers.
- Carry a backpack in which you can store extra clothing, ample drinking water and food, and whatever goodies, like guidebooks, cameras, and binoculars, you might want.
- Most trails on the peninsula have good cell phone coverage. Bring your device, but make sure you've turned it off or got it on the vibrate setting while hiking. There's nothing like a "wake the dead"–loud ring to startle every creature in the vicinity, including fellow hikers.
- Keep children under careful watch. Beachside trails expose young hikers to tempting but dangerous surf, bluff tops can crumble, and animals and plants may harbor danger. Children should carry a plastic whistle; if they become lost, they should stay in one place and blow the whistle to summon help.

Zero Impact

San Francisco's trails are heavily used year-round. We, as trail users and advocates, must be especially vigilant to make sure our passing leaves no lasting mark. Here are some basic guidelines for preserving trails in the region:

- Pack out all your own trash, including biodegradable items like orange peels. You might also pack out garbage left by less considerate hikers.

- Don't approach or feed any wild creatures—the ground squirrel eyeing your snack food is best able to survive if it remains self-reliant.

- Don't pick wildflowers or gather rocks, antlers, feathers, and other treasures along the trail. Removing these items will only take away from the next hiker's backcountry experience.

- Avoid damaging trailside soils and plants by remaining on the established route. This is also a good rule of thumb for avoiding poison oak and stinging nettle, common trailside irritants.

- Don't cut switchbacks, which can promote erosion.

- Be courteous by not making loud noises while hiking.

- Many of these trails are multiuse, which means you'll share them with other hikers, trail runners, mountain bikers, and equestrians. Familiarize yourself with the proper trail etiquette, yielding the trail when appropriate.

- Use outhouses at trailheads or along the trail.

San Francisco Peninsula Boundaries

The boundaries of the San Francisco Peninsula are not geographically fixed. For the purposes of this guide, hikes are listed from the tip of San Francisco at the Golden Gate south to various points on the peninsula in San Mateo County. Along the bay shoreline (east side), the boundary is the San Mateo County line. Along the Pacific shoreline (west side), hikes reach to Pescadero, south of Half Moon Bay. Highway 84 and Pescadero Creek Road form the southern boundary line.

For hikes south of the San Mateo County line, Pescadero, and Highway 84, check out *Best Easy Day Hikes San
Jose,* which covers the South Bay and Santa Clara County.

Land Management

The following government organizations and departments
manage most of the public lands described in this guide.
They can provide further information on these hikes and
other trails in their service areas.

- California State Parks, Department of Parks and Recreation, 416 Ninth Street, Sacramento (mailing address:
  P.O. Box 942896, Sacramento 94296); (916) 653-6995
  or (800) 777-0369; www.parks.ca.gov; info@parks.ca
  .gov. A complete listing of state parks, including those
  in the Bay Area, is available on the Web site, along with
  park brochures and maps.

- Golden Gate National Parks, Building 201, Fort Mason,
  San Francisco 94123-0022; (415) 561-4700; www.nps
  .gov/goga. The Golden Gate National Recreation Area
  (GGNRA) oversees a number of sites on the peninsula
  and in San Francisco proper, including the Coastal Trail
  at Lands End, the Portola Discovery Site on Sweeney
  Ridge, and Milagra Ridge. The Web site contains a
  wealth of information on all sites in the recreation area,
  including downloadable brochures and maps. You can
  also visit any of the visitor centers for more information.

- Golden Gate National Parks Conservancy and Trails
  Forever, Building 201, Fort Mason, San Francisco
  94123; (415) 561-3000; www.parksconservancy.org.
  This is yet another great Internet resource for information on parks and trails in the GGNRA.

- Midpeninsula Regional Open Space District, 330 Distel Circle, Los Altos 94022-1404; (650) 691-1200; www .openspace.org; info@openspace.org. Open space parks dot the peninsula from south of the San Francisco city limits into Santa Clara County. Visit the Web site for specific park information and maps.

- Presidio of San Francisco, Golden Gate National Recreation Area, Building 201, Fort Mason, San Francisco 94123; William Penn Mott Jr. Visitor Center phone: (415) 561-4323; www.nps.gov/prsf.

- San Mateo County Department of Parks, 455 County Center, Fourth Floor, Redwood City 94063-1646; (650) 363-4020; fwww.eparks.net. The county park Web site is a good source of information. Note that no pets of any kind are allowed in county parks.

A number of regional trails span the peninsula, including the San Francisco Bay Trail (baytrail.abag.ca.gov), which follows the bayshore; the Bay Area Ridge Trail (www.ridgetrail.org), which cruises ridgetops around the bay; the Coastal Trail (www.nps.gov/goga; www.california coastaltrail.info), running down the Pacific oceanfront; and the Juan Bautista de Anza National Historic Trail (www.nps.gov/juba), which begins in Nogales, Arizona, and ends in San Francisco. Visit the Web sites for more information.

Public Transportation

A number of bus, rail, and ferry services link communities in the San Francisco Bay Area. For general public transit information and links to specific transit sites, visit 511.org or call 511 from anywhere in the San Francisco metropolitan area.

MUNI, San Francisco's municipal transportation service, offers rail and bus transportation throughout the city. It can be reached by calling 311 in San Francisco or (415) 701-2311 outside the city. The Web site is www.sfmta.com.

Golden Gate Transit also serves the area; call 511 (toll free in the Bay Area) or (415) 455-2000 outside the Bay Area. The Web site is www.goldengate.org.

Ferry services include Golden Gate Ferry, the Blue and Gold Fleet, and East Bay Ferries. Information for Golden Gate Ferry, which serves the North Bay, is at www.golden gateferry.org. The number for schedule information is (415) 555-2000. The address is 1011 Anderson Drive, San Rafael 94901.

Information for the Blue and Gold Fleet, which travels from San Francisco's Pier 39 to Angel Island, Vallejo, the East Bay, and the North Bay, is at www.blueandgoldfleet .com. The main offices are located on Pier 39; call (415) 705-8200 for more information.

Information for East Bay Ferries is available at www .eastbayferry.com. The phone number for the Alameda/ Oakland ferry is (510) 749-4972; write to the ferry service manager at 950 West Mall Square, Alameda 94501. Alameda's Harbor Bay Ferry, the southernmost East Bay ferry, can be reached by calling (510) 769-5500.

For information about Bay Area Rapid Transit (BART) trains, which serve the peninsula and East Bay, visit the Web site at www.bart.gov. Phone numbers vary depending on the area of service and are listed on the Web site. For customer service call (510) 464-7134 or write P.O. Box 12688, Oakland 94604-2688.

How to Use This Guide

No tricks here—this guide is designed to be simple and easy to use. The at-a-glance information at the beginning of each hike includes a short description, the hike distance in miles and type of trail (loop or out and back), the time required for an average hiker, the trail surface, the best season for hiking the trail, other trail users, whether dogs are allowed on the hike, applicable fees or permits, park hours, sources of additional maps, trail contacts for additional information, and any special considerations. Directions to the trailhead are also provided, along with a general description of what you'll see along the way. A detailed route finder sets forth mileages between significant landmarks along the trail.

Maps

The hikes in this book are easy to follow. The maps provided show each trail, so you won't need to buy extra maps. If you decide to explore farther or go off-trail, however, you'll need more detailed maps. All the hikes in this book are covered by the detailed topographic maps published by the U.S. Geological Survey (USGS)—available through local outdoors shops or by calling (888) ASK-USGS or visiting http://store.usgs.gov. If a park trail map is available, that source is also listed.

Hike Selection

This guide describes trails that are accessible to every hiker. The hikes themselves are generally no longer than 5.0 miles round-trip, and some are considerably shorter. They range in difficulty from short, flat excursions perfect for a family outing to ascents up some of the peninsula's most visible peaks and ridges. While these trails are among the best, keep in mind that nearby trails, often in the same park, may offer longer or shorter options better suited to your needs.

Difficulty Ratings

These are all easy hikes, but easy is a relative term. Some would argue that no hike involving any kind of climbing is easy, but in the Bay Area, hills are a fact of life. To aid in the selection of a hike that suits particular needs and abilities, the hikes in this guide are rated easy, moderate, or more challenging. Bear in mind that even the more difficult hikes can be made easier by hiking within your limits and taking rests when you need them.

- **Easy** hikes are generally short and flat, taking no longer than an hour to complete.
- **Moderate** hikes involve increased distance and relatively gentle changes in elevation and will take one to two hours to complete.
- **More Challenging** hikes feature some steep stretches and generally take longer than two hours to complete.

These are completely subjective ratings. Keep in mind that what you think is easy is entirely dependent on your level of fitness and the adequacy of your gear (primarily shoes). If you are hiking with a group, you should select a hike with a rating that's appropriate for the least fit and prepared in your party.

Approximate hiking times are also included, based on the assumption that on flat ground, most walkers average 2 miles per hour. Adjust that rate by the steepness of the terrain and your level of fitness (subtract time if you're an aerobic animal and add time if you're hiking with kids), and you have a ballpark hiking duration. Be sure to add more time if you plan to picnic or take part in other activities like bird watching or photography.

Trail Finder

Best Hikes for Beach/Coast Lovers

1   Golden Gate Promenade
4   Coastal Trail at Lands End
12 Blufftop Tour
19 Sequoia–Audubon Trail

Best Hikes for Children

5   Lobos Creek Boardwalk
6   Stow Lake Loop

Best Hikes for Dogs

1   Golden Gate Promenade
7   Sunset Trail at Fort Funston

Best Hikes for Peak Baggers

8   Summit Trail Loop
18 Mount Ellen Summit Trail

Best Hikes for Great Views

1   Golden Gate Promenade
3   Coastal Trail Battery Tour
4   Coastal Trail at Lands End
8   Summit Trail Loop
10 Portola Discovery Site on Sweeney Ridge
11 Brooks Creek Falls Loop
12 Blufftop Tour

Best Hikes for Nature Lovers

5   Lobos Creek Boardwalk
8   Summit Trail Loop
9   Milagra Ridge
12 Blufftop Tour
19 Sequoia–Audubon Trail

Map Legend

⟦90⟧	Interstate Highway
⟦30⟧	U.S. Highway
⟦20⟧	State Highway
⟦41⟧	Local/Forest Roads
= = = =	Unimproved Road
- - - - - - -	Trail
▬▬▬▬▬	Featured Route
⁔ ⁔	Marsh/Swamp
▭	County and State Forest/Park
▭	National Forest/National Park
⌣	Bridge
⛰	Campground
❓	Information
🅿	Parking
▲	Peak
⊞	Picnic Area
■	Point of Interest/Other Trailhead
⚏	Restroom
⟳	Spring
➏	Trailhead
≋	Waterfall
⬙	Viewpoint
✈	Airport
N ⬇	True North (Magnetic North is approximately 15.5° East)

1 Golden Gate Promenade (Golden Gate National Recreation Area)

Stretched between the towers of the Golden Gate Bridge and the stately homes of San Francisco's Marina District, the Golden Gate Promenade parallels the beach and bayshore, passes along historic Crissy Field, sports awesome views, and is a premiere people-watching venue.

Distance: 3.4 miles out and back

Approximate hiking time: 2 hours

Difficulty: Easy

Trail surface: Asphalt and concrete with an adjacent gravel path

Best season: Year-round. Expect wind and fog to blow in and out through the nearby Golden Gate at any time.

Other trail users: Runners, bicyclists, skaters, skateboarders

Canine compatibility: Leashed dogs permitted

Fees and permits: No fees or permits required

Schedule: Dawn to dusk daily

Maps: USGS: San Francisco North; Golden Gate National Recreation Area brochure and map

Trail contacts: Golden Gate National Recreation Area, Building 201, Fort Mason, San Francisco 94123; (415) 561-4323; www.nps.gov/goga Golden Gate National Parks Conservancy and Trails Forever, Building 201, Fort Mason, San Francisco 94123; (415) 561-3000; www.parksconser vancy.org

Special considerations: This trail can be congested, especially on sunny days. Please be considerate. Though dogs are required to be on leashes, owners allow their animals to run unrestrained on Crissy Field's lawns.

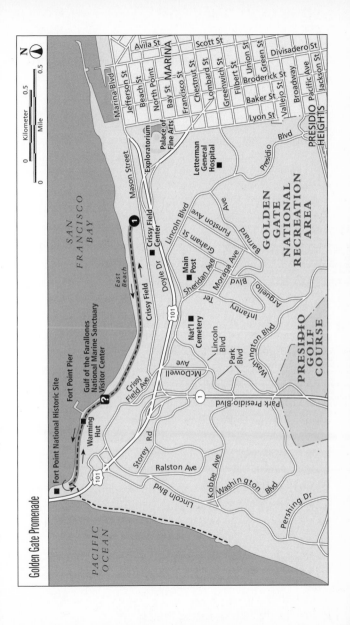

Golden Gate Promenade

N

0   0.5
Kilometer

0   0.5
Mile

PACIFIC OCEAN

SAN FRANCISCO BAY

Fort Point National Historic Site

Fort Point Pier

Warming Hut

Gulf of the Farallones National Marine Sanctuary Visitor Center

East Beach

Mason Street

Crissy Field Center

Exploratorium

Palace of Fine Arts

MARINA

Avila St
Scott St
Jefferson St
Beach St
North Point
Bay St
Francisco St
Chestnut St
Lombard St
Greenwich St
Filbert St
Union St
Green St
Divisadero St
Marina Blvd
Baker St
Broderick St
Lyon St
Vallejo St
Broadway
Pacific Ave
Jackson St

PRESIDIO HEIGHTS

Presidio Blvd

Letterman General Hospital

GOLDEN GATE NATIONAL RECREATION AREA

Lincoln Blvd
Doyle Dr
Crissy Field
Crissy Field Ave

Barnard
Funston Ave
Lincoln Ave
Graham St
Main Post
Sheridan Ave
Moraga Ave
Arguello Blvd
Infantry Ter
Nat'l Cemetery
McDowell Ave
Lincoln Blvd
Park Blvd
Washington Blvd
Park Presidio Blvd

PRESIDIO GOLF COURSE

Storey Rd
Ralston Ave
Kobbe Ave
Washington Blvd
Lincoln Blvd
Pershing Dr

101

1

Finding the trailhead: The East Beach parking area is off Mason Street, less that 0.1 mile east of the intersection of Mason and Marina Boulevard. From Marina Boulevard heading westbound, stay straight at the intersection with Doyle Drive (U.S. Highway 101/ Golden Gate Bridge approach). From Doyle Drive heading south from the Golden Gate Bridge, merge onto Marina Boulevard. At the first stop sign, turn right, make a U-turn, and return to Marina Boulevard. Turn left on Marina and head into the park. *DeLorme: Northern California Atlas & Gazetteer:* Page 104 B2. GPS for the East Beach parking area trail access: N37 48.349 / W122 27.019.

The Hike

More often than not, a blanket of fog creeps in overnight to cover the bay and its city. In the morning the curtain of sea mist pulls back slowly under the warming sun, first revealing sailboats close in to shore, then the dark bulks of Angel and Alcatraz Islands, and finally the red span of the Golden Gate Bridge and the steep Marin Headlands. Whether you've seen it a thousand times or you are a newcomer to the Bay Area, you'll be mesmerized. And one of the best places to watch is from the Golden Gate Promenade.

This wide, flat multiuse trail traces the bayshore from the Marina District to Fort Point and is invariably crowded with hikers, runners, moms and dads pushing strollers, cyclists, folks in wheelchairs, and dog walkers. The dogs, which are supposed to be on leashes, dash in and out of the surf and across the path willy-nilly. Sailboarders and kayakers launch from the beach, mingling with sailboats on sunny, windy days. Even if the fog doesn't burn off, the promenade puts on a show.

Heading west along the path, a trail breaks off to the left (south) to the Crissy Field Center. You can use this cutoff to link up with a paved path on the south side of the restored marsh, designated for faster travelers on bikes or skates. The restored marsh area begins to the trail's left (south), marked by the first of several interpretive signs. Other social trails branch right (north) to the beach. Concrete benches along the promenade and at the waterside offer opportunities to just sit and watch.

The boardwalk leading to the Golden Gate Overlook breaks off the promenade to the right (north) at 0.6 mile, and a narrow dirt track heads left (south) onto a huge grass-covered platform—a re-creation of the historic Crissy airfield. Crissy Field was a hub of military aviation during the 1920s and 1930s, strategically situated in the Presidio where aviators could get aloft expeditiously and cruise the coastal regions looking for enemy ships that might not be seen from coastal fortifications on land.

The promenade continues west between the field and the waterfront, and the beach slowly gives way to a rockier shoreline. You'll pass the Gulf of the Farallones National Marine Sanctuary Visitor Center at the 1.0-mile mark, which is home to wonderful displays for both viewing and touching, including aquariums full of tidal creatures.

Beyond the sanctuary visitor center, spur trails lead to the West Bluff picnic area, which sports tables, interpretive signs, an amphitheater of concrete risers, and little hillocks that serve as windbreaks.

The Warming Hut and the Fort Point Pier (aka Torpedo Wharf) are at 1.3 miles. The wharf is often crowded with anglers, some of whom bustle from one line to another hoping to snag the "big one," while others seem content to use their poles as an excuse to take in the great views of the Golden Gate Bridge and Fort Point. The Warming Hut houses a cafe and bookstore, as well as restrooms. Informational and interpretive billboards are stationed around the building. The Coastal Trail breaks off to the left (south) from the west side of the hut, climbing stairs to Battery East and other military fortifications on the west side of the bridge.

The Golden Gate Promenade proper ends at the Warming Hut, but you can continue west on the access road to the Fort Point National Historic Site at 1.7 miles. Located at the end of the rock-faced seawall below the southern terminus of the Golden Gate Bridge, this Civil War–era fort is open for tours on Friday, Saturday, and Sunday and is well worth a visit. Check the Web site at www.nps.gov/fopo or call (415) 561-4395 for more information. Return as you came.

Miles and Directions

0.0   Start by heading west from the East Beach parking area on the paved path toward the Golden Gate Bridge.

0.1   Pass the side trail to the Crissy Field Center and reach the border of the marsh.

0.2   Cross a bridge that spans the marsh's outlet stream.

0.6   Pass the boardwalk to the Golden Gate Overlook; the trail parallels Crissy Field.

1.0   Pass the Gulf of the Farallones National Marine Sanctuary Visitor Center.

1.3   Arrive at the Warming Hut and Fort Point Pier.

1.7   Reach Fort Point and the end of the line. Retrace your steps to the trailhead.

3.4   Arrive back at East Beach and the parking area.

2 Ecology Trail and Lover's Lane (Presidio of San Francisco)

Located in the heart of the historic Presidio of San Francisco, this route lifts you to a scenic overlook and immerses you in history as it passes by charming homes once occupied by military men and their families.

Distance: 2.3-mile loop
Approximate hiking time: 1.5 hours
Difficulty: Moderate due to the trail's length and some climbing
Trail surface: Dirt singletrack, pavement, sidewalk
Best season: Year-round
Other trail users: Mountain bikers, trail runners
Canine compatibility: Leashed dogs permitted
Fees and permits: No fees or permits required
Schedule: Sunrise to sunset daily
Maps: USGS: San Francisco North; Golden Gate National Recreation Area brochure and map
Trail contacts: Presidio of San Francisco, Golden Gate National Recreation Area, Building 201, Fort Mason, San Francisco

94123; (415) 561-4323; www.nps.gov/prsf
Golden Gate National Parks Conservancy and Trails Forever, Building 201, Fort Mason, San Francisco 94123; (415) 561-3000; www.parksconservancy.org
Special considerations: Social trails intertwine in the woodlands at a couple of locations along the Ecology Trail, which muddies mileage estimates and makes giving specific directions a challenge. No worries: You really can't get lost here, as development encroaches on all sides. But bringing a map, such as the one in this guide or available at the visitor center, can help keep you headed in the right direction.

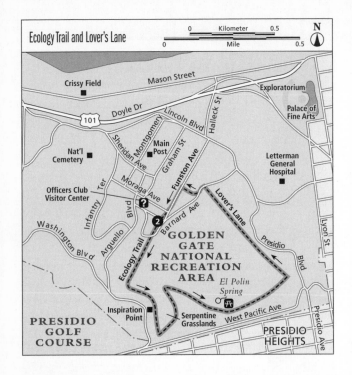

Ecology Trail and Lover's Lane

Crissy Field
Mason Street
Exploratorium
Palace of Fine Arts
Doyle Dr
101
Lincoln Blvd
Halleck St
Sheridan Ave
Montgomery
Main Post
Graham St
Funston Ave
Letterman General Hospital
Nat'l Cemetery
Moraga Ave
Officers Club Visitor Center
Infantry Ter
Arguello Blvd
Barnard Ave
Lover's Lane
Washington Blvd
Ecology Trail
GOLDEN GATE NATIONAL RECREATION AREA
El Polin Spring
Presidio Blvd
Lyon St
Inspiration Point
Serpentine Grasslands
West Pacific Ave
Presidio Ave
PRESIDIO GOLF COURSE
PRESIDIO HEIGHTS

Kilometer 0.5
Mile 0.5
N

Additional information: The Presidio's William Penn Mott Jr. Visitor Center, on the Main Post, is closed. There is a temporary visitor center in the Presidio's Officers Club, located at the south end of Pershing Square on Moraga Avenue.

Finding the trailhead: The trailhead is just south of the Presidio's Main Post. From Mason Street along the Golden Gate Promenade, turn left (south) onto Halleck Street and drive under Doyle Drive to Lincoln Boulevard. Turn right (west) onto Lincoln and proceed several blocks to Montgomery Street. Turn left onto Montgomery and travel south to its intersection with Moraga Avenue. Turn left (east) onto Moraga and drive to its end, where it intersects Funston Avenue. A right on Funston drops you south another block to the trailhead and parking area at Funston and Hardie Avenues, behind Pershing Hall. *DeLorme: Northern California Atlas & Gazetteer:* Page 104 B2. GPS for the parking area at the temporary visitor center in the Officers Club: N37 47.866 / W122 27.529; GPS for the trailhead at Funston and Hardie: N37 47.799 / W122 27.478.

The Hike

The Ecology Trail and Lover's Lane capture the scenic and historic diversity of the Presidio in a neat package. They track through a dark forest of eucalyptus, pine, and cypress to wide vistas at Inspiration Point and showcase both a pocket of rare original habitat and a historical lane that linked the Spanish Presidio to Mission Dolores.

The hike is also a bit of a workout and presents a route-finding challenge—social trails collide in confusing tangles above El Polin Spring and around the Ecology Trail's intersection with Lover's Lane. The area is small enough and developed enough that you won't get dangerously lost, but it can be confusing. Consult a map to keep on track.

Begin by passing through a gate. Initially paved, the trail soon turns to dirt and climbs into a stand of eucalyptus. Stay left (southwest) on the main track, ascending through a dense mixed evergreen forest. The first 0.25 mile or so presents a rather vigorous ascent before the pitch eases in a redwood grove. A social trail drops off to the left (north); stay right (southeast) on the Ecology Trail.

At 0.4 mile you'll enter a pocket of the serpentine grasslands that once covered this area. The flora includes eleven rare and endangered plants, such as Presidio clarkia and Marin dwarf flax. Climb through the restoration zone, staying right at trail intersections, to a brief but steep staircase that leads to the overlook at Inspiration Point.

A broad flagstone platform outfitted with benches and banked with interpretive signs, Inspiration Point offers views across the Presidio's treetops to San Francisco Bay, Alcatraz Island, and Angel Island. One of the signs describes the trees that fringe the view: More than 100,000 trees, mostly nonnatives, were planted on the Presidio as part of a beautification project in the 1800s. The forest is lovely, but the juxtaposition of the trees with the tiny patch of reclaimed serpentine grassland spilling from the vista point is jarring. It's difficult to imagine that before the arrival of Europeans, the grassland predominated.

Return to the Ecology Trail and climb toward the south boundary of the park. Switchback left (north) on a wide path that drops steeply to the base of the serpentine grassland area, then into the El Polin Spring picnic area at 1.2 miles. The spring is located near the head of the hollow and was a water source for the Spanish and Mexican forces at the Presidio.

Climb eastward out of the riparian zone around the spring, past the Julius Kahn Playground and Paul Goode Field, then into a mixed forest of eucalyptus and Monterey pine. In less than 0.5 mile you'll arrive on Lover's Lane, marked by light poles and cutting a straight shot northwest toward the Main Post.

Bordered on the east by stands of eucalyptus and on the west by a row of homes once occupied by officers, enlisted men, and their families, the trail surface changes from dirt to pavement. Though this is a busy corner of the Presidio, it's still possible to imagine what it may have been like to stroll arm in arm with a sweetheart on the narrow path. A quaint brick footbridge spans El Polin Creek at the end of the lane at Presidio Boulevard. The houses of Officers Row, some of the oldest structures on the Presidio, line Funston Avenue on the walk back to the trailhead.

Miles and Directions

0.0   Start in the lot behind Pershing Hall, next to the interpretive sign.

0.4   Reach the restored serpentine grasslands. Stay right (south) at the trail intersections, heading uphill toward the overlook at Inspiration Point.

0.5   Arrive at the overlook and enjoy the views, then continue south toward the park boundary.

0.9   At the trail intersection turn sharply left, switchbacking north on a wide unsigned path that drops to the base of the serpentine grassland. Stay straight (down and north), dropping to the second trail that breaks off to the right (east) toward El Polin Spring. (Note: If you take the first right, you will pass above the spring and picnic area, traveling on sandy paths for about 0.2 mile before reconnecting with the route to Lover's Lane.)

1.2   Arrive at the El Polin Spring picnic area. Stay eastbound on the trail, climbing up past the Julius Kahn Playground and the Paul Goode ball field. Proceed through the woodlands toward Lover's Lane, ignoring social trails that break off right (south) to the park's boundary.

1.6   Reach Lover's Lane. Turn left and follow the lane northwest toward Pershing Square.

1.8   Cross Liggett Street.

2.0   Cross McArthur Street.

2.1   Cross the footbridge over El Polin Creek and climb to Presidio Boulevard. Go left (northwest) on Presidio, then left (southwest) on Funston Avenue. Follow Funston back toward the start of the Ecology Trail.

2.3   Arrive back at the trailhead and parking area.

3 Coastal Trail Battery Tour (Golden Gate National Recreation Area)

The hulking remnants of obsolete military batteries challenge spectacular views, a popular beach, and the Golden Gate Bridge for dominance along this stretch of the Coastal Trail.

Distance: 3.6 miles out and back
Approximate hiking time: 2 hours
Difficulty: Moderate due to length
Trail surface: Dirt singletrack, pavement
Best season: Year-round. The weather can be cold, foggy, and windy, so dress in layers.
Other trail users: Trail runners
Canine compatibility: Leashed dogs permitted
Fees and permits: No fees or permits required
Schedule: Open sunrise to sunset daily
Maps: USGS: San Francisco North; Golden Gate National Recreation Area brochure and map
Trail contacts: Golden Gate National Recreation Area, Building 201, Fort Mason, San Francisco 94123; (415) 561-4323; www.nps.gov/goga
Golden Gate National Parks Conservancy and Trails Forever, Building 201, Fort Mason, San Francisco 94123; (415) 561-3000; www.parksconservancy.org
Special considerations: A portion of Baker Beach is clothing optional. There's no formal boundary between the G-rated and R-rated areas, but the northeast side of the beach, beyond Battery Chamberlin, is "clothing optional."

The surf at Baker Beach is dangerous, so beachgoers are advised not to swim. Facilities include picnic tables, restrooms, barbecue grills, and drinking water.

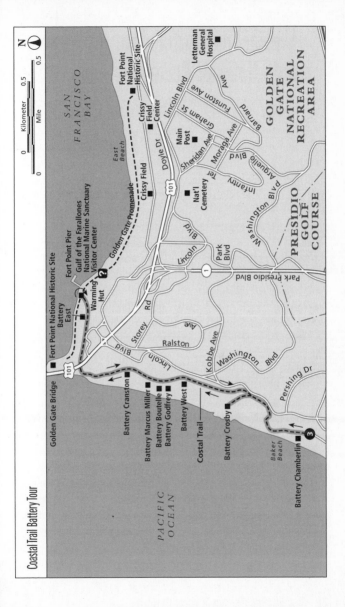

Coastal Trail Battery Tour

N

PACIFIC OCEAN

SAN FRANCISCO BAY

GOLDEN GATE NATIONAL RECREATION AREA

PRESIDIO GOLF COURSE

Golden Gate Bridge

Fort Point National Historic Site

Fort Point Pier

Gulf of the Farallones National Marine Sanctuary Visitor Center

Warming Hut

Battery East

Golden Gate Promenade

Crissy Field

Crissy Field Center

Fort Point National Historic Site

Letterman General Hospital

East Beach

Doyle Dr

Lincoln Blvd

Graham St

Funston Ave

Main Post

Sheridan Ave

Moraga Blvd

Barnard

Nat'l Cemetery

Infantry Ter

Arguello Blvd

Park Blvd

Lincoln Blvd

Washington Blvd

Battery Cranston

Battery Marcus Miller

Battery Boutelle

Battery Godfrey

Battery West

Costal Trail

Battery Crosby

Kobbe Ave

Storey Ave

Ralston

Pershing Dr

Baker Beach

Battery Chamberlin

Park Presidio Blvd

0   Kilometer   0.5

0   Mile   0.5

Additional information: Battery Chamberlin, located on the southeastern boundary of Baker Beach, is home to the "disappearing gun." The gun is fired on the first Sunday of each month, demonstrating how the recoil pushed the gun back and below a defensive barrier where artillerymen could safely reload it. A small military museum is open the first weekend of the month as well, from 10:00 a.m. to 2:00 p.m. For more information call (415) 561-4323.

Finding the trailhead: To reach the Baker Beach trailhead from U.S. Highway 101 at the Golden Gate Bridge, follow Lincoln Boulevard west and south for 0.9 mile to Bowley Street, which is signed for Baker Beach. Turn right (west) onto Bowley Street and drive down to Gibson Road. Turn right (west) onto Gibson, which drops toward the parking area adjacent to the big brick Presidio Water Treatment Plant. Turn right (north) from Gibson Road onto Battery Chamberlin Road, which empties into a large parking lot. The trailhead is at the north end of the lot at Battery Chamberlin. *DeLorme: Northern California Atlas & Gazetteer:* Page 104 B2. GPS: N37 47.593 / W122 28.984.

The Hike

Generations of coastal defenses line the Coastal Trail between Baker Beach and the Golden Gate. From forts that date back to the Civil War to Nike missile sites, San Francisco's seacoast has seen one style of defense give way to the next over hundreds of years as the art of war evolved.

The batteries along this portion of the Coastal Trail generally predate the great wars of the twentieth century. The brick- and earthworks of Batteries East and West were erected just after the Civil War. These were obsolete by the end of the nineteenth century and were replaced by "modern" fortifications, including Batteries Crosby, Boutelle, and Cranston. The only historic man-made structure along the route that hasn't been rendered obsolete is Golden Gate Bridge, which was built in the 1930s.

Many of the batteries offer unsurpassed views of the coastline, the Marin Headlands, and the Golden Gate. Sunbathing and picnicking on Baker Beach is a great way to start or end the hike. The route can be traveled in either direction but is described here heading north and east from Baker Beach to the Golden Gate Promenade.

Begin by visiting Battery Chamberlin. Chain-link fencing surrounds much of the battery, but the gates are open, allowing you to check out the restored "disappearing" gun. From the battery, drop onto Baker Beach, and walk south to the Coastal Trail, which climbs to the edge of Lincoln Boulevard and follows a dirt singletrack along the roadway.

Battery Crosby, at 0.5 mile and set below the road in fragrant scrub, offers wonderful views of the Golden Gate from its flower-and-weed-filled gun emplacements. Wildflowers are a common sight along the trail, especially in late winter and spring, when the vibrant California poppy blooms.

The trail flattens at about the 1.0-mile mark and passes the brick entryways of Battery West. Next up is Battery Godfrey, with a wide concrete apron that opens onto the Golden Gate and makes a marvelous vista point. An interpretive sign describes San Francisco Bay in the last ice age, when it was a river valley and the Farallon Islands were part of the coastline. Battery Godfrey melds into Battery Boutelle; Batteries Marcus Miller and Cranston follow in quick succession.

Beyond the batteries, the Golden Gate Bridge becomes the primary focus. Follow a paved path left (north, then east), dropping under the roadbed of the bridge. The sound of the cars passing overhead is hollow, muffled, and echoing; the architecture is massive, solid, and insulating. Watch for speeding cyclists.

As you emerge from the shadow of the bridge on the bay side of the Golden Gate, Fort Point comes into view. A brick tunnel opens into the earthworks of Battery East, which date back to the post–Civil War era. A viewing platform at the far end of the fortifications offers grand views of the bay and Golden Gate.

The trail arcs northward and descends a flight of stairs to the Warming Hut and the Golden Gate Promenade at 1.8 miles. Check out the sights, then return as you came.

Miles and Directions

0.0 Start at Battery Chamberlin. After exploring the battery, drop onto Baker Beach and head north to the end of the chain-link fence.

0.2 Pick up the signed Coastal Trail and climb away from Baker Beach. The trail leads up to Lincoln Boulevard and then swings east and north to follow the roadway uphill.

0.5 The trail to Battery Crosby departs to the left (north). Follow a dirt path to the site, explore, then return to the Coastal Trail and continue north.

1.0 Pass a series of social trails that lead to Battery West, overgrown with brambles on the left (north) side of the route.

1.2 After passing through Battery Godfrey, arrive at Battery Boutelle. The trail splits beyond Battery Boutelle; stay left (north) on the main trail, which drops down a flight of steps and passes the shrub-covered aprons of Batteries Marcus Miller and Cranston. (**Option:** Take the right trail to see the curved covered walkway at Battery Marcus Miller, then retrace your steps back to the main route.)

1.5 The Coastal Trail merges with a paved path that leads right (east) onto the pedestrian walkway/bikeway of the Golden Gate Bridge and left (northeast) under the huge iron girders. A trail sign marks the route as part of the Juan Bautista de Anza National Historic Trail and the Bay Area Ridge Trail. Follow the left-hand trail north, then east, dropping down under the roadbed of the bridge.

1.7 The trail forks at an interpretive sign; go left (northeast) and sharply downhill through a picnic area. Walk through the brick tunnel at the southeast end of the picnic area, which opens into Battery East. Stay left (northeast) at the trail intersection beyond the battery.

1.8 Drop down a flight of stairs to the Warming Hut and the Golden Gate Promenade. Retrace your steps to Baker Beach.

3.6 Arrive back at the trailhead.

Options: Once on the Golden Gate Promenade, you can continue east past Crissy Field to explore other areas of the Presidio or go west to tour Fort Point. If you leave a shuttle car at East Beach, you can turn this into a 3.0-mile one-way exploration of both the Coastal Trail and Golden Gate Promenade.

4 Coastal Trail at Lands End (Golden Gate National Recreation Area)

The Coastal Trail at Lands End unfurls along the northwest edge of San Francisco, within sight of the Golden Gate Bridge and the narrow strait that separates Point Lobos from the steep folds of the Marin Headlands.

Distance: 3.2 miles out and back

Approximate hiking time: 2 hours

Difficulty: Easy

Trail surface: Pavement, dirt trail and road, a staircase

Best season: Year-round. Be prepared for cold and windy weather at any time of year.

Other trail users: Trail runners, mountain bikers for the first 0.6 mile

Canine compatibility: Leashed dogs permitted

Fees and permits: No fees or permits required

Schedule: Dawn to dusk daily

Maps: USGS: Point Bonita and San Francisco North; Golden Gate National Recreation Area brochure and map

Trail contacts: Golden Gate National Parks, Building 201, Fort Mason, San Francisco 94123-0022; (415) 561-4700; www.nps.gov/goga

Golden Gate National Parks Conservancy and Trails Forever, Building 201, Fort Mason, San Francisco 94123; (415) 561-3000; www.parksconservancy.org

Special considerations: Remain on trails. Straying off-route may bring you dangerously close to crumbling cliffs and a long fall.

Additional information: As of late summer 2008, trail improvements were ongoing. If the Merrie Way parking area is not open when you visit, you may park at Fort Miley on El Camino Del Mar. Various side trails and short staircases lead down to the trail from the Fort Miley parking lot.

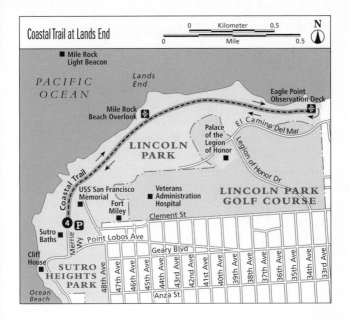

Coastal Trail at Lands End

Finding the trailhead: From U.S. Highway 101 at the Golden Gate Bridge, follow Lincoln Boulevard south, then west, for about 1.5 miles to where it becomes El Camino Del Mar in the upscale neighborhood of Sea Cliff. Continue west on El Camino Del Mar for about 0.9 mile to its intersection with Legion of Honor Drive. Turn left (south), passing the Palace of the Legion of Honor, to Clement Street. Go right (west) on Clement Street for 0.9 mile to its intersection with 48th Avenue and El Camino Del Mar. Go left (south) on El Camino del Mar for less then 0.1 mile to Point Lobos Avenue. Turn right (west) onto Point Lobos Avenue, and then turn right (north) again almost immediately into the Merrie Way parking lot. The trailhead is at the north end of the parking lot. *DeLorme: Northern California Atlas & Gazetteer:* Page 104 B2. GPS: N37 46.863 / W 122 30.706.

The Hike

The Lands End trail follows the route of the Cliff House and Ferries Railway, which at the turn of the twentieth century transported visitors to resort attractions built on Point Lobos by self-made millionaire and one-time San Francisco mayor Adolph Sutro. The former railroad grade supports an impressively scenic trail with unparalleled views of the Golden Gate Bridge, maritime traffic in the strait, and the undulations of the Marin Headlands.

Sutro, who made his fortune in the Nevada silver boom by building a tunnel that ventilated the mines of the Comstock Lode, eventually moved to San Francisco and purchased more than 2,000 acres on the headlands at Point Lobos. He went on to transform some of those holdings into a fabulous resort that included Sutro Baths (now in ruins) and the Cliff House (still thriving). The remnants of what drew thousands to the point in Sutro's day continue to attract thousands more than a century later.

The beauty of trails built on former railroad grades—known as rail trails—is that they are never steep. This is true for the Lands End route, with the exception of a short staircase and some steps at a drop through a gully.

Begin at the north end of the Merrie Way parking lot, heading up on pavement around gentle switchbacks. Within 100 yards of the trailhead, you'll pass the singletrack path down to Sutro Baths, which departs to the left (west). The switchback trail intersects the signed Coastal Trail at 0.1 mile; turn left (north) on the flat, paved route. The parking lot for Fort Miley is above the trail at this intersection. Established in 1901, the fort contains several historic batteries and is well worth a visit. (Note: Although the trail sign notes that it is 1.3 miles to Eagle Point, GPS indicates that it is 1.5 miles to the overlook.)

At 0.2 mile a steep staircase leads up and right (southeast) to the USS *San Francisco* Memorial, and an observation deck on the left (northwest) offers wonderful views out to sea. Continue on the rail trail to another overlook at 0.3 mile. The pavement ends here, but the wide dirt track is easily handled by those on either foot or mountain bike. Mountain bikers may have to dismount to negotiate a short series of log steps that drop into a gully; those on foot will have no difficulty here.

The Veterans Administration Hospital looms over the route at the 0.6-mile mark; it can be reached via either a trail and staircase or a paved access road. Continue on the signed Coastal Trail, which swings past the steep staircase down to the Mile Rock Beach overlook, then reaches its own staircase at 0.8 mile. The fenced-off access to the dangerous Painted Rock cliff is at the foot of the stairs.

Beyond the staircase, the trail reaches back toward the coastline, offering views of China Beach and the extravagant homes of Sea Cliff as it proceeds toward the Golden Gate. Skirt the verdant links of Lincoln Park Golf Course near the Palace of the Legion of Honor before trail's end at the viewing platform at Eagle Point and El Camino Del Mar. Return as you came.

Miles and Directions

0.0 Start at the Merrie Way parking lot trailhead.

0.1 Reach the Coastal Trail proper and turn left (north) onto the paved path.

0.2 Pass the staircase to the USS *San Francisco* Memorial on the right (southeast). A viewing platform on the left offers views of the Golden Gate and the Mile Rock light beacon.

0.3 At the second overlook, the pavement ends. Continue on the dirt track.

0.6 Two intersections—one with a staircase and the second with a paved road—offer access to the Veterans Administration Hospital to the right (south). No bikes are permitted on the trail beyond this point. Stay left (north) on the Coastal Trail.

0.7 Pass the staircase down to the Mile Rock Beach overlook.

0.8 Reach the fenced-off access route to Painted Rocks (heed warning signs against climbing here) and climb the staircase (GPS: N37 47.233 / W122 30.173). The trail resumes its flat, easy demeanor above; stay left to continue along the coastline.

1.0 The trail skirts the fairways of Lincoln Park Golf Course.

1.6 Reach the Eagle Point observation deck and the turnaround point (GPS: N37 47.185 / W122 29.642).

3.2 Arrive back at the Merrie Way trailhead.

Options: Be sure to check out other historical and natural landmarks at Point Lobos. You can explore the remnants of Sutro Baths, where visitors relaxed in great pools filled with ocean water that were enclosed in a greenhouse of stained glass. Enjoy a meal or cocktail in the oft-rebuilt Cliff House, and check out the historic camera obscura. You also can watch sea mammals frolic and sun on Seal Rocks; meander through Sutro Heights, site of Adolph Sutro's extravagant residence, conservatory, and gardens; or head down to nearby Ocean Beach for a sunset stroll.

5 Lobos Creek Boardwalk (Golden Gate National Recreation Area)

Check out a restored coastal dune habitat—which once dominated San Francisco's headlands—along the short, interpretive trail that follows Lobos Creek.

Distance: 0.6-mile loop

Approximate hiking time: 45 minutes

Difficulty: Easy

Trail surface: Boardwalk, dirt singletrack

Best season: Year-round. A visit in each season will reveal different blooms and critters, so come again and again.

Other trail users: None

Canine compatibility: No dogs permitted

Fees and permits: No fees or permits required

Schedule: Open sunrise to sunset daily

Maps: USGS: San Francisco North; Golden Gate National Recreation Area brochure and map

Trail contacts: Golden Gate National Parks, Building 201, Fort Mason, San Francisco 94123-0022; (415) 561-4700; www.nps.gov/goga
Golden Gate National Parks Conservancy and Trails Forever, Building 201, Fort Mason, San Francisco 94123; (415) 561-3000; www.parksconservancy .org

Special considerations: This is a fragile habitat that supports rare and endangered plant species. Please stay on the boardwalk and refrain from collecting blooms or any other artifact.

Additional information: Pick up the *Lobos Creek Dunes Boardwalk Guide,* a full-color interpretive pamphlet with map that is keyed to posts along the trail, at any visitor center in the park.

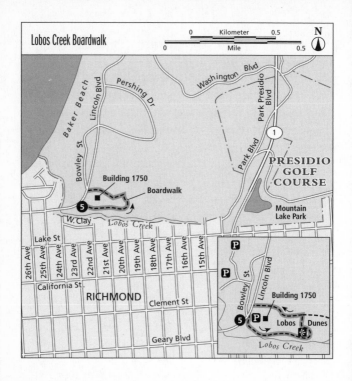

Finding the trailhead: To reach the Lobos Creek Boardwalk trailhead from U.S. Highway 101 at the Golden Gate Bridge, follow Lincoln Boulevard west for 1.3 miles to an unsigned left (southeast) turn into the parking lot of a maintenance facility. The turn is opposite the second Bowley Street entrance to Baker Beach. The trailhead is just inside the entrance, on the south side, at the information billboard. *DeLorme: Northern California Atlas & Gazetteer:* Page 104 B2. GPS: N37 47.308 / W122 28.919.

The Hike

Lobos Creek nourishes a unique habitat, a variety of rare and endangered plant species, and the spirits of those who visit. From the last stand of live oaks thriving in the riparian zone adjacent to the stream to the tiny and rare threespine stickleback that swims in its waters, this is a fertile environment.

A boardwalk meanders out into a coastal dune ecosystem that has been rebuilt and protected in this pocket of the Golden Gate National Recreation Area. The boardwalk parallels the last free-flowing creek in San Francisco, which for years has been the Presidio's drinking water source and now waters beautiful and endangered flora on its northern bank.

Coastal dunes, which once dominated the landscape on San Francisco's headlands, are a difficult place for plants to grow. They shift, they don't hold water well, and they are exposed to almost ceaseless sea breezes. Familiar plants that anchor the ecosystem include silver dune lupine, yellow-blooming bush lupine, scarlet Indian paintbrush, and white and yellow yarrow—a rainbow of blooms that changes as the seasons progress. Among the common you'll also find such rare and endangered natives as dune gilia, San Francisco wallflower, and San Francisco spineflower. Then there's the not-so-rare dune knotweed, which, like the threespine stickleback, deserves mention because of its evocative, irresistible name.

The trail begins in the southwest corner of the parking lot at an interpretive sign. Plants along the boardwalk have been identified with little signs—not that the dragonflies, bees, and songbirds give a hoot about the name of the bloom from which they suck nectar or pillage for bugs to eat. The posh homes of the exclusive Sea Cliff neighborhood rise above the creek on the right (southwest), some tipping on the brink of a notorious slide zone.

The boardwalk heads east through the scrub-covered dunes, with the creek protected by a chain-link fence on the right (south). Numbered posts along the route are keyed to the *Lobos Creek Dunes Boardwalk Guide,* which discusses the valley's history, restoration, and flora and fauna. As the boardwalk arcs northward, the trail forks, and a short branch leads left (west) to a platform surrounded by plants with identification signs. Take as much time as you need to study the blooms, then return to the main boardwalk and continue north to a staircase and trail intersection at the end of the interpretive boardwalk.

Turn left (west) onto the sandy singletrack path, which traces the interface of the dune scrubland and the Presidio Forest, a massive planting from the 1890s that introduced eucalyptus, Monterey pine, and Monterey cypress, completely transforming the landscape. Restoration may someday include removal of these nonnative evergreens. In the meantime, the trail that loops westward behind the maintenance facility rings with birdcall and provides a shady contrast to the dunes.

The path forks just before it reaches Lincoln Boulevard. You can either head straight (west) out to the road and follow the pavement back to the trailhead at about the 0.6-mile mark or go left (southwest) over a wooded rise to the trailhead parking area.

Miles and Directions

0.0 Start at the trailhead on the south side, just inside the entrance to Baker Beach.

0.2 Branch off on a short side path that leads to a viewing platform. Small signs identify the plants that surround the platform.

0.3 Reach the end of the boardwalk and climb into the Presidio Forest.

0.5 Go straight at the fork and follow the pavement back to the trailhead, or turn left and head over a wooded rise.

0.6 Arrive back at the trailhead.

6 Stow Lake Loop (Golden Gate Park)

The easy loop around Stow Lake is a classic Saturday-afternoon stroll for both visitors and residents of San Francisco. Yes, the landscape is lovely and there are fleeting views, but it's the people-watching that makes this short circuit a standout.

Distance: 0.9-mile loop
Approximate hiking time: 45 minutes
Difficulty: Easy
Trail surface: Asphalt
Best season: Year-round
Other trail users: Runners, folks pushing strollers, and wheelchair users
Canine compatibility: Leashed dogs permitted
Fees and permits: No fees or permits required
Schedule: Park open 5:00 a.m. to midnight
Maps: USGS: San Francisco North; maps of Golden Gate Park, including Stow Lake, available online at www.parks.sfgov .org/site/recpark and www .sfgate.com/traveler/acrobat/ maps/1999/ggparkmap.pdf

Trail contacts: San Francisco Recreation and Park Department; (415) 752-0347; www.parks .sfgov.org/site/recpark
Park information also available at www.golden-gate-park.com
Special considerations: Parking close to Stow Lake—or near any attraction in Golden Gate Park for that matter—can be nightmarish on busy weekends. Be patient and willing to walk a bit farther than you otherwise might intend. Parking is available all along Stow Lake, Martin Luther King Jr., and John F. Kennedy Drives.
Additional information: No bikes or skates are permitted on the loop trail. To rent a paddleboat call Stow Lake Boats at (415) 752-0347.

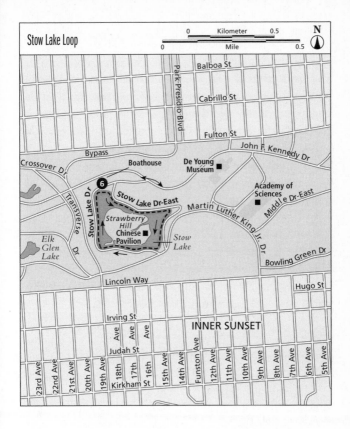

Stow Lake Loop

Finding the trailhead: Access to the Stow Lake boathouse and trailhead can be made from either John F. Kennedy Drive, on the north side of Golden Gate Park, or Martin Luther King Jr. Drive, on the south side of the park. From the intersection of either road with the Crossover Drive (Park Presidio Bypass Drive) within the park, go east to Stow Lake Drive. *DeLorme: Northern California Atlas & Gazetteer:* Page 104 B2. GPS (boat launch): N37 46.236 / W122 28.640.

The Hike

This sweet, short, paved round-we-go in the heart of Golden Gate Park circles Stow Lake and Strawberry Hill. Though sheltered from the cityscape by the thick greenery of the park's landscaping, this is not an escape from the hustle and bustle—it's more a scenic immersion. The people-watching is superlative, and lend an ear; you might hear birdsong but will surely be treated to a symphony of languages from around the world.

Stow Lake is a pea-soup-green doughnut encircling the forested bulk of Strawberry Hill. The paved path circumnavigates the outer shore of the lake, with two bridges spanning the pond from the outer loop to an unpaved inner trail circling the hill. You can jump on the trail at any point, depending on where you find parking on Stow Lake Drive, which forms the outermost ring around the lake.

Since paddleboat tours are a main attraction at Stow Lake, the trail is described traveling clockwise from the boat rental and launch area, which features a snack bar, picnic tables, and restrooms.

The flat path wanders along the lakeshore from the launch to the first bridge to Strawberry Hill; watch for turtles sunning themselves on floating logs and shoreside rocks. Beyond the bridge, the shoreline is more exposed, with families and couples of all ages parked on benches watching passersby on the path and in boats on the water. Some use shady spots under trees to break bread for the ducks and swans that ply the waters.

Circling to the southeast, the red-and-white spires of Sutro Tower pop into view. The panorama of a waterfall and the Chinese Pavilion at the base of Strawberry Hill is much more pleasing—these come into view at about the 0.5-mile mark on the south side of the lake.

At 0.6 mile the circle road drops away from the trail to the left (south) along with a dirt track that leads down to Martin Luther King Jr. Drive. Beyond, you'll pass a second bridge across the water to Strawberry Hill; this one has a stonework facade, more romantic than its counterpart on the opposite side of the lake. Pass a few more benches and enjoy the passing pedestrian traffic before you arrive back at the boat launch and trailhead at 0.9 mile.

Miles and Directions

0.0 Start at the boat rental and launch area.

0.2 Pass the first bridge that arcs over the water to Strawberry Hill. From the bridge you can see a steep trail leading toward the top of the wooded hill. Remain on the obvious paved path around Stow Lake.

0.6 A dirt side trail leads left (south) and down to Martin Luther King Jr. Drive. Continue straight on the lakeside path.

0.8 Reach the second bridge to Strawberry Hill.

0.9 Arrive back at the trailhead.

Option: Cross either of the bridges and explore Strawberry Hill, which features a flat, easy trail that visits the waterfall and pavilion. Golden Gate Park offers other walking tours, including those leading into the Japanese Tea Garden and museum area and out toward Ocean Beach.

7 Sunset Trail at Fort Funston (Golden Gate National Recreation Area)

Sights on the ground and in the sky enliven the Sunset Trail, which leads hikers to historic Battery Davis and overlooks Ocean Beach. The fort is a favorite of hang gliders and dog lovers as well as hikers.

Distance: 2.0 miles out and back

Approximate hiking time: 1 hour

Difficulty: Easy

Trail surface: Pavement, sand

Best season: Year-round

Other trail users: Cyclists, trail runners

Canine compatibility: The leash requirement is generally ignored; dogs mostly run free.

Fees and permits: No fees or permits required

Schedule: Park open 6:00 a.m. to 9:00 p.m. daily

Maps: USGS: San Francisco North; Golden Gate National Recreation Area brochure and map

Trail contacts: Golden Gate National Parks, Building 201, Fort Mason, San Francisco 94123-0022; (415) 561-4700; www.nps.gov/goga
Golden Gate National Parks Conservancy and Trails Forever, Building 201, Fort Mason, San Francisco 94123; (415) 561-3000; www.parksconservancy.org

Special considerations: The surf at Fort Funston—and all along Ocean Beach—hosts dangerous rip currents and unpredictable breakers. Swim, wade, or surf with care.

Given the number of dogs that play in the sand at Fort Funston, dog owners should be diligent about picking up after their pets. If you stray off-trail, watch your step!

The paved portion of the Sunset Trail is suitable for wheelchair users.

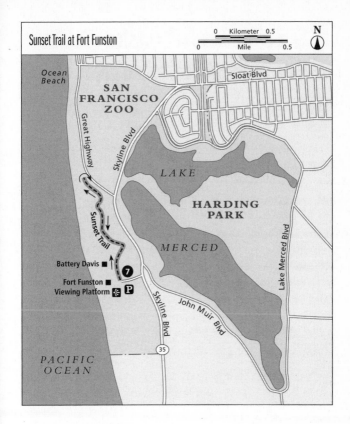

Sunset Trail at Fort Funston

0   Kilometer   0.5
0   Mile   0.5

N

Ocean Beach

SAN FRANCISCO ZOO

Sloat Blvd

Great Highway

Skyline Blvd

LAKE

HARDING PARK

MERCED

Lake Merced Blvd

Sunset Trail

Battery Davis ■

Fort Funston ■
Viewing Platform

7

P

Skyline Blvd

John Muir Blvd

35

PACIFIC OCEAN

Additional information: For hang gliders and those interested in watching the aerial acrobatics, Fort Funston offers great wind, a world-famous intermediate launch site, and a viewing deck that looks out over the dunes and the great kites. The fort also is home to a native plant nursery that has been operating for more than twenty years. The Environmental Education Center is used by school groups and is not open to the public.

Finding the trailhead: Fort Funston is located on Skyline Boulevard at the southern end of the Great Beach, about 4.5 miles south of the Cliff House. The fort's entrance can only be reached from the southbound lanes of Skyline Boulevard and is located about 1.7 miles south of Sloat Boulevard. To reach the fort from the northbound lanes of Skyline Boulevard, make a U-turn at John Muir Drive and head south to the park entrance. *DeLorme: Northern California Atlas & Gazetteer:* Page 104 B2. GPS: N37 42.876 / W122 30.162.

The Hike

Fort Funston hunkers in the windswept dunes at the southern boundary of San Francisco's Ocean Beach. Once a unit in the extensive system of military defenses built along the coastline to protect the valuable port in San Francisco Bay, it's now part of the Golden Gate National Recreation Area and enjoys a second incarnation as a hang-gliding hot spot and a center for canine cavorting.

The sandy Sunset Trail reaches north from the wooden viewing deck where visitors can watch hang gliders launch to World War II–era Battery Davis, its casemated gun emplacements camouflaged by windblown forest and sand. The area's legacy as a military installation lasted into the Cold War, when the fort served as a Nike missile installation; the parking lot is the former launch site.

But even if the hang gliders have folded their wings, historic batteries fail to spark your interest, and your tastes lean more to cats than dogs, the Sunset Trail displays scenic merits difficult to resist. The trail is built on the edge of the dunes, and views sweep north and west across Ocean Beach and the Pacific—particularly dramatic under broken clouds, when the sun shines in spotlights on the ceaselessly moving water.

The trail begins on the western edge of the parking area, near the launch site and viewing platform. Take the paved trail north, passing an informational sign and the overgrown front-side of the battery at 0.1 mile.

The trail curves around the battery's back side, where a picnic area is perched in the shelter of the camouflaging trees. If you've brought Fido along, you'll find water and water dishes here. Near the battery's northern end, the trail splits; stay left on the "high road," passing (or venturing into) the tunnel on the left (west).

The trail drops downhill from the battery, offering views up Ocean Beach, to the point where the two trails that split above merge. A sign marks beach access on the left (west).

The pavement ends at 0.8 mile, but those who are able can continue on the sandy path through the dunes. By now the dogs and crowds have been mostly left behind. You hike with the wind, the sand, the sparse plants that find purchase on the dunes, and wonderful views north of Ocean Beach and distant Point Lobos.

The sand path ends at the 1.0-mile mark at an interpretive sign that discusses the dunes and a trail-closure sign. Turn around and return as you came, taking the "low road" at the bottom of the hill to add variety to the route. This will bring you back up to Battery Davis. Stay right (west) at the trail juncture just below the battery, curving toward the ocean on the paved roadway to the dog-watering area. From here, retrace your steps to the trailhead and parking area.

Miles and Directions

0.0   Start near the hang glider launch site and viewing platform.

0.1   Reach Battery Davis.

0.3   Pass a picnic area on the back side of the battery and a dog-watering station. When the trail splits, stay left on the upper path.

0.6   Trails merge at the base of the hill. A beach access path breaks off to the left (west). Stay straight on the Sunset Trail.

0.8   The pavement ends; continue on the sandy path.

1.0   Reach the end of the trail above the Great Highway and Ocean Beach. Retrace your steps to the trail junction at the bottom of the hill below Battery Davis.

1.4   At the trail junction go left on the paved roadway. (**Option:** Go right and retrace your route all the way back to the trailhead and parking area.)

1.5   At the junction go right (west), curving up to Battery Davis.

1.7   Return to the dog-watering site behind the battery. Retrace your steps back toward the viewing platform and parking area.

2.0   Arrive back at the trailhead.

8 Summit Trail Loop (San Bruno Mountain State and County Park)

On a clear day, panoramic vistas radiate from the flanks of San Bruno Mountain like the glow from the tip of a sparkler. The big bang is the San Francisco skyline, rising white and lively to the north.

Distance: 3.3-mile loop
Approximate hiking time: 2 hours
Difficulty: More challenging due to trail length and a steady climb and descent
Trail surface: Dirt singletrack
Best season: Autumn, when you are least likely to encounter view-obscuring fog, but the trail can be traveled year-round.
Other trail users: Trail runners
Canine compatibility: No dogs permitted
Fees and permits: $5 entry fee per car
Schedule: The park opens daily at 8:00 a.m. and closes at or before sunset, depending on the season. April through Labor Day, the park remains open until 8:00 p.m. November to February, the park closes at 5:00 p.m.

Maps: USGS: San Francisco South; San Bruno Mountain State and County Park brochure and map
Trail contacts: San Mateo County Department of Parks, 455 County Center, Fourth Floor, Redwood City 94603; (650) 363-4020 or (650) 589-4294; www.eparks.net
State parks Web site: www.parks.ca.gov
Special considerations: Fog, rain, and wind can make conditions downright arctic on the summit, so be prepared for changing conditions. Rain can also render the lower portions of the trail muddy.
Additional information: Mountain bikes are allowed on some trails in the park but not on the Summit Trail Loop.

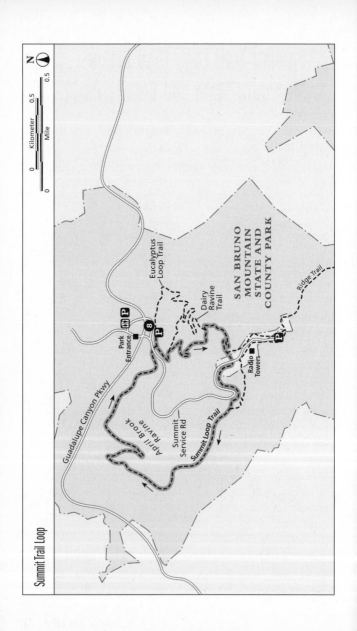

Summit Trail Loop

Finding the trailhead: To reach the trailhead from the northbound lanes of Interstate 280 in Daly City, take the Eastmoor Avenue exit to Junipero Serra Boulevard. Go right (northwest) on San Pedro Road for 0.3 mile to East Market Street. Follow East Market Street, which becomes Guadalupe Canyon Parkway, for 2.2 miles to Radio Road and the entrance to San Bruno Mountain State and County Park on the left (north).

From the southbound lanes of I-280, exit at Eastmoor Avenue and turn left (east) on Eastmoor, heading over the freeway to the intersection with San Pedro Road and Junipero Serra Boulevard. Follow the directions above from this intersection.

From U.S. Highway 101 take the Bayshore Boulevard exit. Head west on Bayshore Boulevard for about 2 miles to the Guadalupe Canyon Parkway. Turn right (west) onto Guadalupe Canyon Parkway and proceed to Radio Road and the park entrance on the right (north).

From the entry kiosk follow the park road past the lower parking area, where you'll find an information billboard, restrooms, trashcans, and picnic tables. The road curves under Guadalupe Canyon Parkway and climbs to a second, upper lot located 0.2 mile from the kiosk. *DeLorme: Northern California Atlas & Gazetteer:* Page 104 B2 and C3. GPS: N37 41.709 / W122 26.056.

The Hike

The views on a clear day from the uppermost reaches of San Bruno Mountain are among the best I've ever seen, spinning in all directions toward sister peaks that boast their own great panoramas—Mount Tamalpais in the north, Mount Diablo to the east, and Montara Mountain to the south.

But say the fog rolls in—a soggy parka that San Bruno Mountain and its surroundings wear with great regularity. When socked in by grayness, attention turns downward and inward. Trails on the mountain become routes for the hiker attentive to tiny blooms and little brown birds flicking into and out of the rich bouquet of coastal scrub that crowds the trail's edge. The scrub includes several varieties of uncommon or endangered manzanita and wildflowers, fragrant sage and other herbs, and prickly blackberries.

Begin the hike at the information billboard describing habitat restoration efforts. You can pick up a trail map here (if you haven't gotten one already). The trail sign lists the Summit Loop Trail at 3.1 miles and also gives distances for shorter hiking options in the park. (FYI: The route described here totals 3.3 miles, probably because of the trail changes at the summit.) Go right (west) on the gravel singletrack, heading into the scrub. At the first trail junction, with the Eucalyptus Loop Trail, go left and up into the eucalyptus grove. The right trail is the end of the Summit loop. As with all loops, you can go either way. The trail is described here clockwise, with a quick and dirty up and a long, relaxed downhill run.

A switchback lifts you into the scrub, and you'll not find much shade on the rest of the climb (which won't matter if the fog's in). At 0.3 mile the Eucalyptus and the Summit Loop Trails part ways. Go right (southeast) on the Summit Loop.

Switchbacks take you back and forth from views of San Francisco Bay and Mount Diablo to the north and east to views west and north across the pastel homes of Daly City and southern San Francisco to the Pacific.

After traversing into and out of Cable Ravine—and serving up awesome views—the singletrack intersects the Dairy Ravine Trail at 0.6 mile. Less that 0.1 mile later you'll reach an overlook and . . . yes . . . more awesome city-from-a-bird's-eye views.

Two quick switchbacks and a ridgetop traverse south toward the summit towers lead to the intersection with the Ridge Trail. Remain on the Summit Trail, which climbs toward the lattice architecture of the tower farm. The summit service road intersects the route at 1.0 mile; the Summit Loop continues across the road behind the gate across private property. This portion of the route is unclear, muddled by fences and poor signage. To ensure easy route-finding, turn right (northwest) on the roadway and head down an easy 0.3 mile to the west face of the mountain and a gated access road on the left (west). The trail, now well signed, continues its downhill run on the right (east) side of the roadway.

The trail descends gently through the lush scrub, then steepens and sweeps around switchbacks into April Brook ravine, crossing its soggy bottom via a wooden bridge. Short boardwalks span the seeps that bleed from the mountainside into the brook as you climb out of the ravine. The trail parallels Guadalupe Canyon Parkway back to the trailhead and parking area.

Miles and Directions

0.0   Start at the information billboard.

0.1   Reach the first trail junction and go left (south and up) on the combined Eucalyptus and Summit Loop Trails.

0.3   The Eucalyptus and Summit Loops diverge. Go right (southeast) on the Summit Trail.

0.4   The trail traverses the south face of a brushy ravine and climbs with the radio towers in sight. The fragrant shrubs are rounded low, hummocked by nearly constant wind from the sea.

0.6 Reach the Dairy Ravine Trail junction. Stay straight (right/east) on the Summit Trail.

0.8 At the intersection with the Ridge Trail, stay right (south) on the Summit Trail toward the tower farm.

1.0 Arrive at the summit service road. A sign indicates that the Summit Trail continues behind the gate across the road, but finding the trail is difficult. Instead turn right (north) and head down the road.

1.3 Reach a gated access road on the left (west). Go around the gate to the continuation of the Summit Trail on the right (northeast).

1.6 Pass a bench.

1.8 Pass a trail marker and a social trail, remaining on the obvious Summit Trail.

2.2 Another social trail leads left (north) to a small rock outcrop; remain right and downhill on the Summit Trail.

2.5 The steepening trail leads down switchbacks to the base of April Brook ravine, where a wooden bridge spans the creek. The trail climbs in a long traverse out of the ravine north toward Guadalupe Canyon Parkway.

2.8 Sweep around the north face of the mountain, climbing parallel to Guadalupe Canyon Parkway over bridges and through copses of oak, Monterey pine, and eucalyptus.

3.1 Cross a final bridge and climb to the summit service road.

3.2 Cross the road to the Eucalyptus and Summit Loop intersection. Go left (northeast) and down on the Summit Loop Trail.

3.3 Arrive at the trailhead and parking area.

9 Milagra Ridge (Golden Gate National Recreation Area)

Winds off the Pacific scour the grassy slopes of Milagra Ridge, a sweet little nugget of wildland in a big bland porridge of tract houses.

Distance: 1.2-mile loop
Approximate hiking time: 1 hour
Difficulty: Easy
Trail surface: Dirt singletrack and paved roads
Best season: Year-round; fog least likely in late summer and fall
Other trail users: Trail runners, mountain bikers
Canine compatibility: Leashed dogs permitted
Fees and permits: No fees or permits required
Schedule: Open sunrise to sunset daily
Maps: USGS: San Francisco South; Golden Gate National Recreation Area Milagra Ridge map and brochure, available online at www.nps.gov/goga and in park visitor centers

Trail contacts: Golden Gate National Recreation Area, Building 201, Fort Mason, San Francisco 94123; (415) 561-4323; www.nps.gov/goga
Golden Gate National Parks Conservancy and Trails Forever, Building 201, Fort Mason, San Francisco 94123; (415) 561-3000; www.parksconservancy.org
Special considerations: Please remain on trails to protect the fragile habitat. Paved trails are wheelchair accessible.
Additional information: To volunteer for restoration programs, contact the GGNRA's Site Stewardship Program at (415) 561-3034, ext. 3437, or visit www.parksconservancy.org.

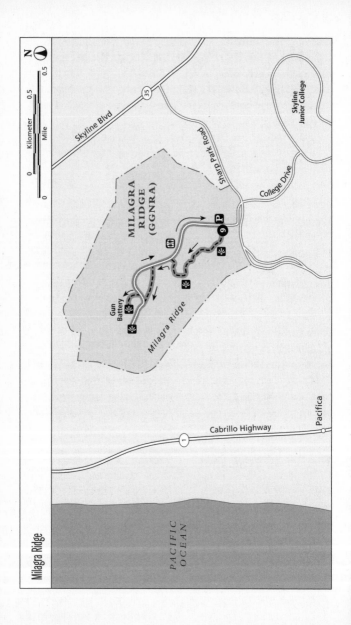

Milagra Ridge

Finding the trailhead: Milagra Ridge can be reached from Skyline Boulevard (Highway 35) or Highway 1 in Pacifica. Heading south from San Francisco, follow Skyline to Sharp Park Road. Turn right (west) and drive 0.6 mile to College Drive. Turn right (north) onto College Drive and continue for 0.2 mile to the end of the road and the trailhead.

From Highway 1 in San Francisco, head south to the Sharp Park Road exit in Pacifica. Go east on Sharp Park Road for 1.5 miles to the intersection with College Drive. Turn left (north) onto College Drive to the trailhead. *DeLorme: Northern California Atlas & Gazetteer:* Page 104 C2. GPS: N37 38.135 / W122 28.461.

The Hike

Park literature calls Milagra Ridge "an island ecosystem," and that's an apt description. Taking in the views from anywhere in the park, development stretches in all directions—a sea of ticky-tacky houses that only find their limit to the west, on the shores of the mighty Pacific.

Given the surroundings and the fact that the open space encompasses less than 250 acres, it's a miracle that the ridge supports such a diversity of plant and animal life. Among the fauna that calls the ridge home are the endangered mission blue butterfly, the San Bruno elfin butterfly, the California red-legged frog, and the San Francisco garter snake.

The ridge is the subject of an ongoing site stewardship program. Sponsored by the park and carried out by a group of dedicated volunteers that include students from area high schools, work to rehabilitate and maintain the natural habitat has been ongoing since the property was acquired in 1984. Also in evidence are the remnants of Milagra's military history, which included construction of a post–World War II–era battery and a Nike missile site.

A network of singletrack trails, paved trails, and a paved road winds through the scrublands on the ridgetop. The loop described here links some of the paths, but if you stray, no worries. The area is simply too small to get lost in.

Begin by mounting stairs on the left (west) side of the road. Climb past a fenced-off covered reservoir on the right (north) to an overlook with great views of the Pacific and the pastel mosaic of the suburbs that surround the ridge. Head north, traversing the ridgetop, to a flight of stairs that drops into a saddle. Veering west again, wander through blooming scrublands to the paved road.

Turn left (west) on the unpaved path that drops westward to another overlook before turning inland again. Pass a lone Monterey cypress—the only tree you'll see along the route—then cross a clearing to the paved road. Go left (west) on the pavement, dropping to an old battery and native plant garden, both of which offer spectacular ocean views. The garden has been planted where a gun once was mounted.

Backtrack up the paved road to a staircase that climbs to a concrete pad at 0.8 mile—yet another spectacular overlook. Head east down the paved road to a footpath that breaks off to the left (northeast); follow the footpath down to its junction with the pavement. Turn left and return to the main paved road at about the 1.0-mile mark, where you'll find a portable restroom, a trash can, and an informational billboard.

Unless you plan to do laps, turn left (south) onto the main paved road, arriving back at the trailhead at 1.2 miles.

Miles and Directions

0.0 Start by heading up the staircase from the roadside parking area. Pass the covered reservoir and head across the ridge.

0.3 Drop down a staircase to the paved road. Turn left (west) onto an unpaved path, walking west to another overlook.

0.6 Meet the paved road again and follow it to the native plant garden and gun battery. Backtrack to the road and climb a staircase toward another overlook.

0.8 Reach the overlook at the concrete pad. Follow paved and unpaved paths back to the main road.

1.0 Drop to the roadway at the restrooms.

1.2 Arrive back at the trailhead.

10 Portola Discovery Site on Sweeney Ridge (Golden Gate National Recreation Area)

Distance: 3.6 miles out and back

Approximate hiking time: 2 hours

Difficulty: More challenging due to the trail's length and a steady climb

Trail surface: Pavement, dirt roadway, and singletrack

Best season: Year-round. Best season for views is fall, when the fog is less likely to roll in.

Other trail users: Mountain bikers, trail runners, equestrians on the ridgetop trails

Canine compatibility: Leashed dogs permitted

Fees and permits: No fees or permits required

Schedule: Open sunrise to sunset daily

Maps: USGS: Montara Mountain; Golden Gate National Recreation Area Sweeney Ridge map and brochure, available online at www.nps.gov/goga and at park visitor centers

Trail contacts: Golden Gate National Recreation Area, Building 201, Fort Mason, San Francisco 94123; (415) 561-4323; www.nps.gov/goga
Golden Gate National Parks Conservancy and Trails Forever, Building 201, Fort Mason, San Francisco 94123; (415) 561-3000; www.parksconservancy.org

Special considerations: Dress in layers to ensure comfort and warmth in changing weather conditions. There are no facilities along the trail or at the trailhead.

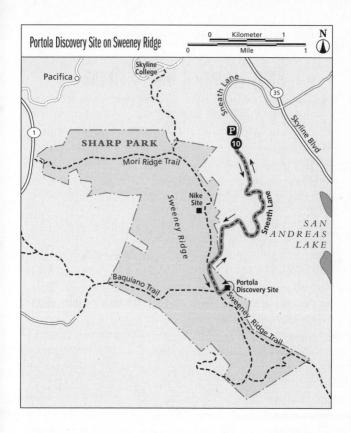

Portola Discovery Site on Sweeney Ridge

Finding the trailhead: Approach the trailhead from the north or south via Skyline Boulevard (Highway 35) in San Bruno. Sneath Lane heads west from Skyline Boulevard, climbing through a residential area for 1.1 miles to the trailhead parking area. There is parking for about fifteen cars at the end of the road. *DeLorme: Northern California Atlas & Gazetteer:* Page 104 C2. GPS: N37 37.139 / W 122 27.248.

The Hike

Explorer Gaspar de Portola, charged by his country to scout settlement sites in California that would cement its status as a Spanish colony, set off from Mexico with missionary Junipero Serra in 1769. Leaving Serra behind to establish a mission in San Diego, Portola headed north, looking for Monterey Bay.

But his expedition, traveling by land, didn't recognize Monterey as the perfect colonial site described by an earlier explorer. So they kept walking. And walking. Finally, on November 4, 1769, the exhausted Portola and his companions climbed Sweeney Ridge to survey the lay of the foreign land. There they beheld the unexpected—a bay of colossal proportions destined to become one of the most important harbors on the California coast. A bay that would one day be the site of a famously cosmopolitan city surrounded by spectacular parklands.

How could he have known?

Though not nearly as pristine as it was in missionary times, San Francisco Bay still presents an amazing vista from the top of Sweeney Ridge at the Portola Discovery Site. Views in all directions are spectacular. Landmarks around the bay are inscribed on a cylinder of granite that tops one of the monuments at the site, enabling visitors to identify all they can see.

Begin the climb to the discovery site with a flat stretch on Sneath Lane. Pass around the gate and head south down the paved road toward the northern reaches of San Andreas Lake, which glitters in the distance. The easy passage ends when the route arcs southwest and begins a long, unbroken ascent to the ridgetop.

You will wind upward on pavement through coastal scrub that frames views of the lake, San Francisco International Airport, and the waters of the bay. Pass the "fog line" at 0.8 mile; beyond this marker, a single yellow line runs up the middle of the road.

The trail swings northwest, climbing at a fairly steep pitch, with San Bruno Mountain rising to the northeast. The steepness mellows as the road heads back southwest and passes through a stand of eucalyptus. A final push, this time heading directly west, lands you atop the ridge at the intersection of Sneath Lane and the Sweeney Ridge Trail.

Leave the pavement for the dirt track that heads south toward the Portola Discovery Site, passing a pair of benches perched on the edge of the trail looking west over the Pacific. The discovery site is less than 0.1 mile from the trail junction, reached via any of the social trails that mount a knob on the east side of the route.

The serpentine monument that commemorates the Portola expedition is on the north side of a little clearing atop the knob. A second monument honoring Carl McCarthy, who escorted more than 11,000 people to the site as part of its preservation effort, is on the opposite side of the clearing and carries the engravings that identify landmarks on the horizon.

When your explorations at the site are complete, return as you came.

Miles and Directions

0.0 Start by heading down the paved road beyond the gate.

0.2 Pass a gated side road.

0.3 Start the long climb to the ridgetop.

0.8 Pass the fog line.

1.3 Travel through a stand of eucalyptus.

1.7 Reach the summit of the ridge and the intersection of Sneath Lane and the Sweeney Ridge Trail. Turn left (south) on the unpaved Sweeney Ridge Trail. The paved road to the north leads to water towers and the remains of a Nike missile site.

1.8 Take in the views from the Portola Discovery Site. The Baquiano Trail drops off the ridge to the west. Retrace your steps.

3.6 Arrive back at the trailhead.

Options: If ever an area begged for further exploration, it would be Sweeney Ridge. Aside from the discovery site, you can head north along the ridge to the Nike missile site or west toward the Pacific on either the Baquiano or Mori Ridge Trail.

11 Brooks Creek Falls Loop (San Pedro Valley County Park)

Travel into the Brooks Creek drainage and you'll explore a landscape little changed since the days of Spanish missionaries and explorers. On the downhill run, views of the Pacific Coast enliven switchbacks that drop down Montara Mountain.

Distance: 2.5-mile loop
Approximate hiking time: 1.5 hours
Difficulty: More challenging due to the trail's length, a steady climb at the outset, and switchbacks on the descent
Trail surface: Dirt singletrack
Best season: Year-round; fall optimal for enjoying the trail without fog
Other trail users: Trail runners
Canine compatibility: No dogs permitted
Fees and permits: $5 fee
Schedule: The park opens daily at 8:00 a.m. and closes at or before sunset, depending on the season. April through Labor Day, the park remains open until 8:00 p.m. November through February, the park closes at 5:00 p.m.

Maps: USGS: Montara Mountain; San Pedro Valley County Park brochure and map available online at www.eparks.net and at the trailhead
Trail contacts: San Pedro Valley County Park, 600 Oddstad Boulevard, Pacifica 94044; (650) 355-8289
San Mateo County Department of Parks, 455 County Center, Fourth Floor, Redwood City 94063; (650) 363-4020; www.eparks.net
Additional information: The park's visitor center, open from 10:00 a.m. to 4:00 p.m. on weekends and holidays, offers interpretive displays, a bookstore, and a library. Picnic areas can be reserved by contacting the park in advance.

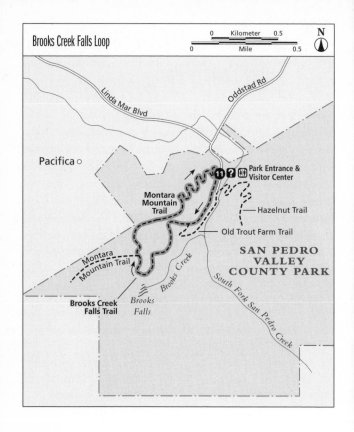

Brooks Creek Falls Loop

0 Kilometer 0.5

0 Mile 0.5

N

Linda Mar Blvd

Oddstad Rd

Pacifica ○

11 ❓ 🚻 Park Entrance & Visitor Center

Montara Mountain Trail

Hazelnut Trail

Old Trout Farm Trail

SAN PEDRO VALLEY COUNTY PARK

Montara Mountain Trail

Brooks Creek

South Fork San Pedro Creek

Brooks Creek Falls Trail

Brooks Falls

Finding the trailhead: To reach the park from Highway 1 in Pacifica, go east on Linda Mar Boulevard for 1.9 miles to its end at Oddstad Road. Turn right (south) onto Oddstad Road and go 1 block to the park entrance on the left (east). Park in the lot near the visitor center. The trailhead is located behind the Old Trout Farm restrooms, where you'll also find trash cans and water. *DeLorme: Northern California Atlas & Gazetteer:* Page 104 C2. GPS: N37 34.688 / W122 28.558.

The Hike

Ocean breezes are a mainstay in Pacifica, cooling even the hottest summer days and regularly blowing fog over the tract houses that line the hillsides. That nearly constant moisture supports the lush coastal scrub that pillows the lower slopes of Montara Mountain and feeds San Pedro Creek and Brooks Creek, which flow through alder and willow to the San Pedro Valley floor.

The park preserves a site of historical significance. In 1769 Don Gaspar de Portola's colonial expedition overshot its desired destination, Monterey Bay, and happened instead upon another enormous body of water, San Francisco Bay. Part of Portola's exploration of the area included a visit to the lush, fruitful San Pedro Valley. After Mission Dolores was established on the bayshore, the oceanside valley became an important supply outpost, providing food and cattle for the mission.

The eucalyptus growing around the foot of the ridge also links back to historical times. The quick-growing Australian natives were commonly planted as windbreaks on coastal farms and ranches. The Old Trout Farm Trail is named for—you guessed it—a trout farm that operated on the valley floor into the early 1960s.

The Brooks Creek Falls loop, which includes a portion of the Montara Mountain Trail, begins behind the Old Trout Farm restroom in the southwestern corner of the parking lot. It climbs steadily through mixed forest and coastal scrub, leaving the Old Trout Farm Trail behind near the bottom of a eucalyptus-shaded hollow.

Tracing the Brooks Creek drainage, the creek can be heard, if not seen, as it cascades down a tree-clogged bed.

Near the midpoint of the ascent, you'll be treated to views of Brooks Creek Falls, a 175-foot spill that is full in the winter months and has usually dried up by early summer. Even in autumn, however, you can spy the water stain on the rocks at the head of the steep ravine. You can also watch broad-winged birds—crows, hawks, and turkey vultures—ride the thermals generated in the sheltered valley. It's an ability you'll envy as you trudge uphill on foot.

Climb through scrub along the southeast face of the Brooks Creek drainage, then arc south and west via switchbacks to the Montara Mountain Trail at 1.2 miles. It's all downhill from here, as the trail drops northward along a ridge. Views open periodically of Pacifica and the Pacific. The cotton-ball clusters of lace lichen that hang from the limbs of manzanita and oak are indicators of the cleanliness of the air on the mountain.

On the lower reaches of the ridge, a eucalyptus forest shades the trail, with switchbacks leading from ocean views amid scrub to no views in the woods. More than a half dozen switchbacks later, you'll reach the park's paved service road, which is just above the trailhead. A short hop through a last stand of eucalyptus, and you are back in the parking lot.

Miles and Directions

0.0 Start behind the restrooms and the picnic area. At the trail junction go left (south) on the Old Trout Farm Trail (also the Brooks Creek Falls Trail).

0.1 Pass a trail marker amid ferns, poison oak, fir, oaks, and eucalyptus.

0.3 Reach a closed trail that departs to the left; stay right (south) on the Old Trout Farm Trail. About 50 feet beyond stay right (south) again on the Brooks Creek Falls Trail. The Old Trout Farm Trail drops down to the left.

0.5 Cross the moist head of a ravine at a couple of posts; this may involve negotiating water in the winter months.

0.7 Leave the forest for scrubland, traversing up the slope above the creek amid red-barked manzanita.

0.8 Cross a bridge over a gully.

0.9 The waterfall comes into view at an open patch in the trail, where a bench offers a comfortable viewing perch. Round a few switchbacks as the trail swings first south, then west, and then flattens atop the ridge.

1.2 Arrive at the Montara Mountain Trail junction, where a bench offers a chance to rest and take in the views of Pacifica and the ocean beyond. Go right (north) on the Montara Mountain Trail, starting the descent.

1.3 Pass a "pullout" with a bench just before the first of many switchbacks.

1.5 Reach the first stately eucalyptus.

1.7 Now in the eucalyptus forest proper, the trail splits, with the upper route leading to a viewing bench. Unless you want to take in the sights, stay left on the lower track. Seven switchbacks moderate the descent below.

2.5 Arrive at the paved park service road and a trail sign. Cross the road and follow the path down to the first trail junction behind the Old Trout Farm restrooms. Go left and down to the trailhead and parking area.

Options: The park offers several other trail options, including a 0.1-mile nature trail; the Weiler Ranch Road Trail, which is open to cyclists; and the Valley View Trail, which explores the heights on the southeastern ridge of the valley.

12 Blufftop Tour (James V. Fitzgerald Marine Reserve)

This scenic trail along the bluffs overlooking the Pacific traces the terrestrial boundary of a marine reserve famed for its tidepooling and for sightings of sea mammals such as seals and sea lions. From the bungalows of Seal Cove to the views from Pillar Point, the route is a delight.

Distance: 4.5 miles out and back

Approximate hiking time: 2.5 hours

Difficulty: Moderate due to length

Trail surface: 10-foot-wide dirt and gravel trail, a short stretch on pavement

Best season: Year-round; fall is your best bet for a fog-free day.

Other trail users: Mountain bikers, trail runners

Canine compatibility: Leashed dogs permitted outside the boundaries of the reserve

Fees and permits: No fees or permits required

Schedule: Marine reserve open from 8:00 a.m. daily; closes 5:00 p.m. in winter, 8:00 p.m. in summer, 7:00 p.m. in spring and fall

Maps: USGS: Montara Mountain OE W; James V. Fitzgerald Marine Reserve map on the San Mateo County Parks Web site at www.eparks.net

Trail contacts: Friends of Fitzgerald Marine Reserve, P.O. Box 451, Moss Beach 94038; (650) 728-3584; www.fitzgeraldreserve.org San Mateo County Department of Parks, 455 County Center, Fourth Floor, Redwood City 94063; (650) 573-2592; www.eparks.net

Special considerations: Tidepooling is a major activity at the reserve during low tides. Though this trail keeps hikers above the shoreline on the bluff, there are opportunities to add a stretch along the tide line to the hike.

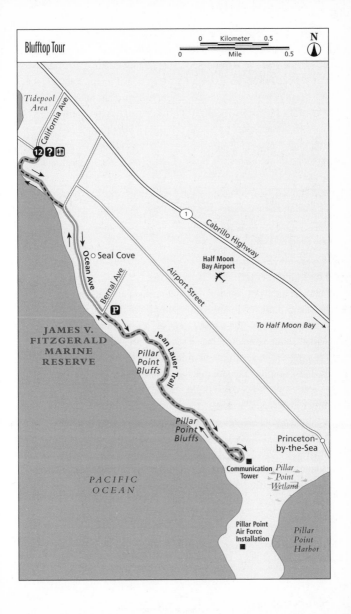

Blufftop Tour

0   Kilometer   0.5
0   Mile   0.5

N

Tidepool Area

California Ave

12 ? 👫

1 Cabrillo Highway

Half Moon Bay Airport

Seal Cove

Ocean Ave

Bernal Ave

Airport Street

To Half Moon Bay

P

JAMES V. FITZGERALD MARINE RESERVE

Jean Lauer Trail

Pillar Point Bluffs

Pillar Point Bluffs

Princeton-by-the-Sea

Communication Tower

Pillar Point Wetland

PACIFIC OCEAN

Pillar Point Air Force Installation

Pillar Point Harbor

Consult a tide chart (published online and in many Bay Area newspapers) if you want to add this activity to your visit. Tidepools contain many fragile and exotic creatures. Please observe proper etiquette when exploring. Tread lightly and carefully to avoid crushing tidal residents. Leave all sea life undisturbed—collecting, turning, or moving starfish, mussels, limpets, and other animals threatens their survival.

Additional information: The reserve hosts educational programs for adults and school groups. For information on tours or events, visit the Friends of Fitzgerald Marine Reserve Web site at www.fitzgeraldreserve.org. The Jean Lauer Trail is wheelchair accessible, as are several of the side trails that intersect on the bluff, including the access trails from the Bernal Road and Airport Road trailheads.

Finding the trailhead: From Highway 1 in Moss Beach south of Pacifica, turn right (west) onto California Avenue. Follow California Avenue 0.3 mile to the reserve parking lot at the end of the road at North Lake Street. The parking lot is on the right (north), with a small visitor center, restrooms, picnic tables, and trash and recycle bins. The trailhead is at the corner of North Lake Street and California Avenue, near the tsunami evacuation route sign.

A second trailhead is located on Airport Road at the southeast end of the Peninsula Open Space Trust property. To reach this small lot, with parking for ten cars, a restroom, and an informational sign, turn right (west) off Highway 1 onto Cypress Avenue (just south of California Avenue). Turn left (south) onto Airport Road and continue for 0.9 mile to the trailhead. *DeLorme: Northern California Atlas & Gazetteer:* Page 104 D2. GPS: N37 31.412 / W122 30.949.

The Hike

No natural interface is as dramatic as that between the land and the sea. The boundary's dynamics add an element of danger to its exploration, for though tides are predictable, waves are not. The blufftop trail overlooking the meeting place of earth and water in the Fitzgerald Marine Reserve bears witness to how volatile the zone is.

While rich tidepools and a craggy shoreline are the reserve's main attractions, the blufftop trail that meanders south has many merits, including expansive views in all directions, fragrant and colorful coastal scrub, and the opportunity to contemplate which of the charming bungalows in Seal Cove you'd most like to buy . . . if you had a million dollars.

The hike begins by crossing San Vicente Creek, then climbs into the cypress forest that shades much of the reserve property. Stay right at all trail intersections to an overlook of the tidepooling area and beach. Hitch a bit farther up and then head south through the forest, staying alongside the fence that guards the cliff edge to better enjoy the seaside views.

The trail enters the neighborhoods of Seal Cove near the 0.5-mile mark, meandering along seafront streets lined with cottages that are guaranteed to inspire coast-living envy in the staunchest mountain man. Pass the historic Moss Beach Distillery restaurant, then follow the heaving pavement of Ocean Avenue to the boundary of Pillar Point Bluff open space, owned by the Peninsula Open Space Trust.

On the blufftop you'll share the trail with cyclists and dogs, some off-leash despite the leash law. The great white ball on Pillar Point is part of an Air Force installation and is the dominant landmark from this point on.

Braided trails that once crisscrossed the blufftop were removed in fall 2008. A new 10- to 12-foot-wide trail— the Jean Lauer Trail—was installed, side trails were moved inland from the bluff's edge, and the surrounding area was reseeded with native vegetation. This section of the route is also part of the Californai Coastal Trail, and several side trails—also rehabilitated—intersect the Lauer trail. Improvements include construction of a new trailhead and parking area off Airport Road near the southeastern boundary of the property. Route-finding is simple. As the ranger at the reserve advised, "If you keep the ocean on one side and Highway 1 on the other, you can't lose your way"

Crest the blufftop on the Lauer trail and the sparkling waters of Pillar Point Harbor come into view. Half Moon Bay Airport, built by the U.S. Navy during World War II and now used by private planes, ranges along Highway 1 to the east. The Pacific Ocean pounds the cliffs on the west.

Near its end above lovely Pillar Point Marsh, where more than 150 plant and animal species abide, the trail loops back to return north to the Fitzgerald reserve. You cannot reach the restrooms, parking, and beach access at the Pillar Point Harbor trailhead without crossing private property, so remain on the Jean Lauer Trail

On the return journey, watch the water for seals and sea lions playing. A bit farther out to sea, you may be able to spot a migrating gray whale.

Miles and Directions

0.0 Start by crossing San Vicente Creek on a metal bridge.

0.1 Reach the tidepool overlook and then climb into the cypress forest. Stay to the right (west) along the fenceline through the trees.

0.3 At the trail junction go right (south) on the gravel path. You can see the homes of Seal Cove ahead.

0.4 Reach the reserve boundary at the intersection of Beach Way and Cypress Avenue. Stay right (straight/south) on Beach to Marine Boulevard, then stay right (west) on Beach Way. A block farther, at Orval Avenue, roadside benches offer viewing opportunities for trail users and residents alike. Drop to the Moss Beach Distillery parking lot. You can either follow Los Banos Avenue to Ocean Avenue or traverse the parking lot to Ocean Avenue, which is closed to vehicle traffic.

0.7 Climb rough pavement up Ocean Avenue, then continue south past the charming home fronts.

1.0 Ocean Avenue ends at Bernal Avenue. The trailhead to the Lauer trail is about 100 yards east on Bernal Avenue, with an informational kiosk. Continue on to the Pillar Point Bluffs.

1.3 Continue south on the dirt trail as Highway 1 and the coastal mountains come into view to the east.

1.7 The trail offers views down to the gold sand of a crescent beach below the Pillar Point Air Force installation.

2.3 Reach the south end of the trail above the Pillar Point Harbor trailhead. A parking lot, restrooms, and the West Shoreline beach access are below but cannot be accessed without crossing private property. Turn around and retrace your steps on the Lauer trail to return to the marine reserve; or take one of the new side trails that loop back to the lauer trail.

3.5 Arrive back at the Bernal Avenue trailhead in Seal Cove; retrace your steps from here back to the reserve.

4.5 Reach the trailhead and parking area.

Options: The extremely short trail to the tidepooling area begins at the intersection of North Lake and Nevada Avenues, on the northwest edge of the reserve parking lot. The trail is lined with interpretive signs and drops directly to the rocky shore, where you can check out the starfish, anemones, limpets, and barnacles until the tide washes over them once again.

13 Sawyer Camp Trail

Snaking through the San Andreas Fault's rift valley, the Sawyer Camp Trail is one of the classic easy hikes on the San Francisco Peninsula. From the dam at San Andreas Lake to the Jepson Laurel, the path accommodates and satisfies thousands of visitors each year.

Distance: 5.0 miles out and back

Approximate hiking time: 2.5 hours

Difficulty: Moderate, due only to the distance

Trail surface: Pavement

Best season: Year-round

Other trail users: Cyclists, trail runners, skaters

Canine compatibility: No dogs permitted

Fees and permits: No fees or permits required

Schedule: Sunrise to sunset daily

Maps: USGS: San Mateo; Crystal Springs Trail map and guide published by the San Mateo County Department of Parks and available at the trailhead

Trail contacts: San Mateo County Department of Parks, 455 County Center, Fourth Floor, Redwood City 94063; (650) 363-4020; www.eparks.net. Contact park rangers for the Crystal Springs Trail by calling (650) 589-4294. The trail runs through the Peninsula Watershed of the San Francisco Public Utilities Commission; (415) 544-3289; sfwater.org.

Special considerations: This is rattlesnake and wildcat country, believe it or not. Protect yourself from these animals by staying on the trail, avoiding travel at sunrise and sunset, and traveling with a hiking partner.

Finding the trailhead: From the southbound lanes of Interstate 280 in Millbrae, take the Millbrae Avenue exit. Pass under the freeway and follow the frontage road back north to Hillcrest Boulevard. Turn left (west) on Hillcrest Boulevard and pass back under the free-

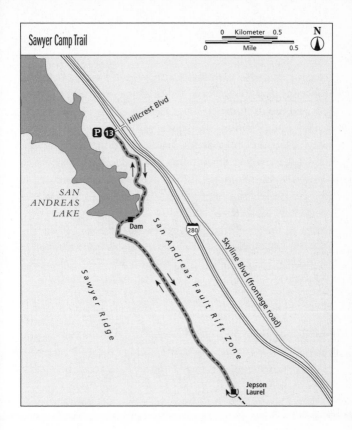

way to parking alongside the roadway. From the northbound lanes of I-280, take the Millbrae Avenue/Larkspur Drive exit. Follow the frontage road north to Hillcrest Boulevard and turn left (west) under the freeway to park alongside the roadway. The Crystal Springs Trail intersects Hillcrest at its end; the trailhead for the Sawyer Camp segment is to the left (south) as you face the coastal mountains. *DeLorme: Northern California Atlas & Gazetteer:* Page 104 D2. GPS: W37 35.336 / N122 24.787.

The Hike

The Sawyer Camp Trail is like your dream guy or gal in trail form—smart, athletic, really good-looking, and, to top it off, just plain nice. No wonder thousands of people hike, bike, or run on it each year.

What's the attraction? Start with the geology: It sits smack atop the San Andreas Fault, the notorious crack in the earth whose 1906 rupture was a defining moment in San Francisco's colorful history. Rocks on one side of the valley differ drastically from those on the other, as they ride on entirely separate tectonic plates.

Then there's the natural history: The Jepson Laurel, the largest laurel in the state of California, enjoys a sun-splashed dotage at the end of the hike described here. It's a gnarly, tumbledown specimen, fenced off to protect its ancient, delicate root system. But when you read its vital statistics, which were recorded in 1923 on a stone plaque (at the time it was only the second-largest laurel in the state), you can't help but be impressed. Measuring 22 feet 4 inches in circumference and standing 55 feet tall, it was, and still is, impressive.

Though the laurel dwarfs other plant life and wildlife in the area, some of these smaller creatures are rare and exotic as well. The Peninsula Watershed's 23,000 acres are home to more than 250 different animal species, including the endangered San Francisco garter snake, and a plethora of insects, including the blue elfin butterfly.

The watershed doesn't slack off in the human history department. Gaspar de Portola, the Spanish explorer who set out to find Monterey Bay in 1769 and instead found the much more impressive (and daunting) San Francisco Bay, camped in the area; the plaque at the trailhead memorializes this event. The trail was named for Leander Sawyer, who, according to the trail brochure, had a camp near the Jepson Laurel. The route also served as the main thoroughfare between San Francisco and Half Moon Bay for a time.

And if that weren't enough, there's the trail itself: an easy ramble on a paved track in the shade of overarching bay laurels and stately oaks. It has only one minor hill, which leads to and from the San Andreas Lake dam. Otherwise the trail rolls along the valley floor below the lake, with the breath of the not-so-distant Pacific washing over forested Sawyer Ridge to the west. It's just all-around pleasant.

It's also very straightforward. After an inauspicious start, adjacent to the noisy interstate on a path adorned with a power station, power poles, and a sign warning about rattlesnakes, you'll drop to the dam and the lovely lake at the 0.5-mile mark. Cross to the west side of the rift valley, then cruise through the woods past a couple of picnic areas to the Jepson Laurel, where you'll find restrooms, more picnic tables, benches, trash cans, and water. This is the turnaround point, but you can continue south to Lower Crystal Springs Reservoir and beyond, if you choose. Otherwise, return as you came.

Miles and Directions

- **0.0** Start at the trailhead behind the gate on the south side of Hillcrest Boulevard's cul-de-sac.
- **0.2** Climb the paved road past a power station to an informational billboard and a water fountain.
- **0.3** The trail descends past a gated road on the left (south). Sweeping curves drop past a bench toward the shimmer of San Andreas Lake.

0.5 Pass a mile marker and signs that denote the area as a state fish and game refuge.

0.8 Arrive on flat land at the east end of the San Andreas Lake dam. There's a porta-potty here.

1.0 Cross the dam, passing a plaque describing the San Andreas Fault. On the west side of the lake, another plaque commemorates the dam's completion in 1960. The trail turns left (south), following the rift valley.

1.3 The trail wanders through a quieter world, where your accompaniments are hawks' cries and the rustle of creatures in the underbrush.

1.5 Pass a bench and a mile marker.

1.7 A small picnic area and benches are tucked into a lovely laurel grove on the right (west) side of the trail.

2.0 After passing another bench and picnic ground—this one in an oak grove—reach another mile marker.

2.5 Arrive at the Jepson Laurel, where you'll find the laurel itself, informational signs, picnic tables, restrooms, and other facilities. Unless you plan to follow the trail farther south, retrace your steps to the trailhead.

5.0 Arrive back at the roadside parking area on Hillcrest Boulevard and trail's end.

Options: The Sawyer Camp Trail is part of the larger Crystal Springs Trail system, which extends from San Bruno in the north to Huddart County Park in the south and includes links into Edgewater County Park and Preserve. The Sawyer Camp Trail is 6.0 miles long in its entirety and reaches south to Lower Crystal Springs Reservoir. There's much more to do in the rift valley, so take your time and explore.

14 Sylvan Trail Exercise Loop (Edgewood County Park and Preserve)

After a long climb, the top of the Sylvan Trail opens onto rolling slopes where wildflowers raise their colorful heads in salute to the sun. The sight, especially in spring, will make you forget that you are exercising.

Distance: 2.5-mile loop

Approximate hiking time: 1.5 hours

Difficulty: Moderate due to the trail's length and steady climb and descent

Trail surface: Dirt singletrack

Best season: Year-round; spring and early summer best for wildflower viewing

Other trail users: Trail runners; horses allowed on the Edgewood Trail but not on the Sylvan Trail Exercise Loop

Canine compatibility: Dogs not permitted

Fees and permits: No fees or permits required

Schedule: The park opens daily at 8:00 a.m. and closes at or before sunset, depending on the season. April through Labor Day, the park remains open until 8:00 p.m. November through February, the park closes at 5:00 p.m.

Maps: USGS: San Francisco South; Edgewood County Park and Preserve brochure and map

Trail contact: San Mateo County Department of Parks, 455 County Center, Fourth Floor, Redwood City 94063; (650) 363-4020; www.eparks.net
Edgewood County Park and Preserve: (650) 368-6238

Special considerations: Stay on the trail to avoid contact with poison oak. Please don't pick the wildflowers—leave them in place for others to enjoy and so they can bloom again next year.

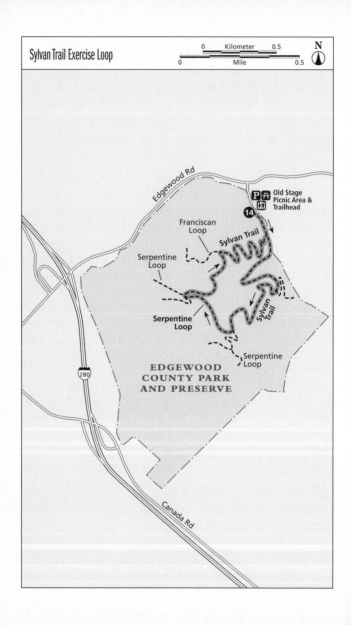

Sylvan Trail Exercise Loop

0   Kilometer   0.5

0   Mile   0.5

N

Edgewood Rd

Old Stage
Picnic Area &
Trailhead

14

Franciscan
Loop

Sylvan Trail

Serpentine
Loop

Serpentine Loop

Sylvan Trail

Serpentine
Loop

EDGEWOOD
COUNTY PARK
AND PRESERVE

280

Canada Rd

Finding the trailhead: The park is located at 10 Old Stagecoach Road in Redwood City. From Interstate 280 take the Edgewood Road exit. Go east on Edgewood Road and follow it 0.7 mile to the park entrance at Old Stagecoach Road. One parking lot is alongside Edgewood Road and filters into the park via a wooden bridge and boardwalk. The main lot is just down Old Stagecoach Road. The Sylvan Trail Exercise Loop trailhead is at the southern end of the main parking area. *DeLorme: Northern California Atlas & Gazetteer:* Page 114 A3. GPS (roadside parking lot): N37 28.373 / W122 16.676.

The Hike

The list of native and endangered flowers that bloom on the upper slopes of Edgewood County Park and Preserve is impressive. Farewell-to-spring, yellow and clay-colored Mariposa lilies, sticky monkey flower, Ithuriel's spear and Franciscan onion, globe lily and tidy tips, blue dicks and buttercups . . . check out the postings on the billboard in the parking lot and the labeled plantings at the park entrance to get some idea of what you'll encounter on your trip into the preserve.

All this loveliness, plus a good workout, awaits you on the Sylvan Trail Exercise Loop, which leads up a well-maintained dirt path to the top of an 800-foot ridge, then switchbacks down through oak woodlands to the trailhead again.

Begin the loop at the Old Stage picnic area just south of the parking lot. A paved trail traces the side of the green, leading up to picnic tables and restrooms that are just right (west) of the Sylvan trail marker.

Head left (south) on the Sylvan Trail Exercise Loop, which climbs through poison oak–infested scrub along a slope above neighborhood homes. After passing the returning portion of the loop at 0.3 mile, the singletrack sweeps west into a gully, traversing a sunny south-facing slope. A small bridge crosses a seasonal stream; cross a second stream, then a more substantial third, and the path arcs onto the north wall of the ravine, now shrouded in shady oaks.

Views open of the East Bay hills and houses on hillsides closer in as you round a series of switchbacks at about 0.8 mile. In the grassy sections along this part of trail, enjoy a preview of what's to come above, whether that's a wild-flower display or a sea of golden grasses burned crispy by the endless summer sun.

A right (northwest) turn at the 1.0-mile mark leads to a traverse of a wooded hillside, then a climb onto grassy slopes where wildflowers thrive. You are in the thick of it upon arriving at the junction of the Serpentine and Franciscan Trails at 1.3 miles. The views aren't bad either, especially as you curve eastward on the exercise loop and gaze down on the bay and the salt evaporation ponds that line its south-western shores.

The trail generally descends from this point, passing a second intersection with the Franciscan Loop at 1.7 miles. The murmur of the nearby freeway is a minor distraction as you round eight switchbacks and the views disappear. The loop ends at 2.3 miles on the trail behind the neighbor-hood. It's a quick downhill run to the left (north) back to the trailhead.

Miles and Directions

0.0 Start at the southern end of the main parking area.

0.3 Cross a drainage ditch and pass a social trail that heads left into a neighborhood.

0.4 Reach the intersection with the return leg of the Sylvan

Loop. Stay left (south), heading toward the Serpentine Loop.

0.5 Cross a series of seasonal streams and arc through the head of the ravine to a mile marker. Continue climbing along the north-facing slope.

0.8 Views north and east of nearby homes and the distant East Bay hills open and improve as you climb through woodland and grassland.

1.0 Pass a mile marker. At the trail intersection in a saddle about 50 feet ahead, turn right (northwest) on the signed Sylvan Trail Exercise Loop; the sign also indicates this is part of the Serpentine Loop.

1.3 Arrive at the junction of the Franciscan and Serpentine Loop Trails. A short climb leads to the ridgetop, where you can enjoy views down into the I-280 corridor. Turn right (east) onto the Serpentine/Sylvan Trail.

1.5 Pass a mile marker on the grassy, flowery slope.

1.7 Reach a junction with the Franciscan Loop. Go right (east) and downhill on the Sylvan Trail.

2.0 Switchbacks descend past a mile marker.

2.3 Reach the junction with the first part of the loop. Turn left (north) and retrace your steps to the Old Stage picnic area.

2.5 Arrive at the picnic area and trailhead.

15 Old Barn Trail (Burleigh Murray Ranch State Park)

Most of San Francisco's "hidden gems" have long been sussed out, but Burleigh Murray Ranch State Park, just east of Half Moon Bay, remains a bit obscure and underutilized. Come for the peace, come for the quiet, come to revisit ranching days long gone at the old barn at trail's end.

Distance: 2.4 miles out and back
Approximate hiking time: 1.5 hours
Difficulty: Easy
Trail surface: Gravel ranch road
Best season: Year-round; wildflowers at their peak in spring
Other trail users: Trail runners
Canine compatibility: Dogs not permitted
Fees and permits: No fees or permits required

Schedule: Park open 8:00 a.m. to sunset
Maps: USGS: Half Moon Bay; California State Parks Web site map at www.parks.ca.gov
Trail contact: California State Parks, 1416 Ninth Street, Sacramento 95814 (mailing address: P.O. Box 942896, Sacramento 94296); (650) 726-8819; www.parks.ca.gov

Finding the trailhead: Burleigh Murray Ranch State Park is located just south and east of Half Moon Bay. From the Cabrillo Highway (Highway 1) northbound or southbound, turn east onto Higgins Purisima Road (at the fire station). Follow Higgins Purisima Road, which becomes Higgins Canyon Road, for 1.7 miles to the park gate and small parking area on the left (east). *DeLorme: Northern California Atlas & Gazetteer:* Page 114 A2. GPS: N37 26.693 / W122 24.172.

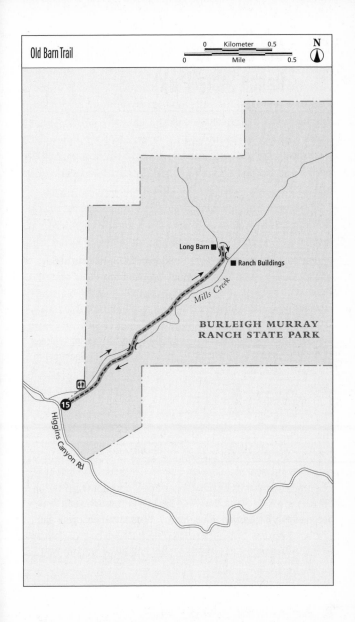

0   Kilometer   0.5

0   Mile   0.5

N

Long Barn ■

■ Ranch Buildings

Mills Creek

BURLEIGH MURRAY
RANCH STATE PARK

15

Higgins Canyon Rd

The Hike

Ranching along California's coast has a long tradition. It began in the earliest colonial times with the arrival of padre Junipero Serra and his missionary expedition in 1769. When the Mexican government ceded California to the United States nearly one hundred years later, many of the state's sprawling ranchos were transferred to American cattlemen, who operated dairy farms up and down the rugged coastline.

Burleigh Murray Ranch was one of those farms, purchased in the 1860s by a British glazier named Robert Mills (for whom Mills Creek is named). The ranch passed from father to son to grandson, and shortly after the death of Mills's descendant Burleigh H. Murray in the late 1970s, more that 1,300 acres and historic buildings were donated to the California State Parks system. The park has since added parcels to the property, which stretches eastward toward Highway 35 on the east side of the Santa Cruz Mountains.

The park remains relatively undeveloped, with a single trail leading to the historic dairy barn and water tanks beyond. The 200-foot-long barn, showpiece of the park, is one of only a few of its kind in the United States. It housed not only cows but also immigrant workers from Ireland, Portugal, and other European countries. These days the long barn, built in 1882 of locally harvested redwood and fir, is shored up against the hill it was built into, a design that made it easy to load hay into the loft from a road built at the second-floor level. A portion of the barn's stone foundation is exposed, rusted farm implements are scattered about its exterior, and its dark interior is lit by sunlight filtered through gaps in the siding.

To reach the barn and the other ranch buildings, which are used as park residences and off-limits to visitors, begin at the interpretive panel in the parking lot. Slip past the gate and head up the broad ranch road. It's a mostly gentle ascent, first through grasslands with Mills Creek hidden in willow, alder, and oak to the left (north). Steep hills, including Miramontes Ridge on the north, cradle the creek valley. Stands of eucalyptus and overgrown meadows are interspersed along the route.

Cross Mills Creek on a wooden bridge shaded by eucalyptus near the halfway point of the climb. A glance over the edge of the bridge reveals the dark, clear water below, flowing past the concrete buttresses. Continue more steeply upward beyond the bridge, with the creek now on your right (south) and large eucalyptus creaking in the wind overhead.

The route continues to pass through alternating open areas and fragrant eucalyptus groves, where leaves spin down like random helicopter rotors to litter the roadway. Pass a picnic table and trash can in a grove before the trail turns sharply north at the junction with the access road to the Burleigh Murray firearms range (off-limits to the public). The trail splits about 100 yards beyond, with the right (upper) road leading to park residences (also off-limits) and the left (lower) road leading to the historic barn.

At the barn you'll find a cluster of picnic tables and an informational billboard that describes the barn's construction and life on the ranch. When you've rested, eaten, and edified yourself, retrace your steps to the trailhead.

Miles and Directions

0.0 Start at the small parking area on Higgins Canyon Road.

0.1 Pass a porta-potty on the left (north) and continue up the ranch road. Mills Creek is on the left (north).

0.4 Cross the bridge over Mills Creek. There is another restroom here. The trail steepens as it continues northeast.

0.9 Pass a picnic table and trash can in a eucalyptus grove.

1.1 Reach the junction with the access road to the Burleigh Murray firearms range and go left (north) on the main trail. The trail splits 100 yards beyond; stay left on the lower road. The right (upper) road leads to park employee residences. (Note: Both the firearms range and employee residences are off limits.)

1.2 Cross a bridge and arrive at the long barn. Retrace your steps.

2.4 Arrive back at the trailhead and parking area.

Option: The ranch road continues up the Mills Creek drainage from the long barn, eventually reaching some water tanks. When visited in late summer 2008, it was not well maintained and obviously little used.

16 Crystal Springs/Toyon Camp Road Loop (Huddart County Park)

Calming, cooling redwood groves shade much of this long loop. A uniquely north-coast phenomenon, the redwoods weave a lofty canopy that filters and softens even the harshest summer sun.

Distance: 3.8-mile loop

Approximate hiking time: 2 hours

Difficulty: More challenging due to distance and steady climbing

Trail surface: Dirt singletrack, broken pavement on an access road

Best season: Year-round

Other trail users: Trail runners, equestrians, automobiles on the Toyon Camp Road, on portions of the Crystal Springs Trail and the Dean Trail

Canine compatibility: No dogs permitted

Fees and permits: $5 per vehicle

Schedule: 8:00 a.m. to sunset. From April to Labor Day, the park is open until 8:00 p.m. November to February, the park closes at 5:00 p.m.

Maps: USGS: Woodside; Huddart County park map and brochure

Trail contacts: San Mateo County Department of Parks, 455 County Center Fourth Floor, Redwood City 94063-1646; (650) 363-4020; www.eparks .net; Huddart County Park direct line: (650) 851-0326

Special considerations: Stay on the trail to avoid contact with poison oak.

Additional information: Huddart County Park offers a variety of amenities, including camping and picnic facilities, sand volleyball, and barbecues. To reserve a campsite or group picnic area, call (650) 363-4021.

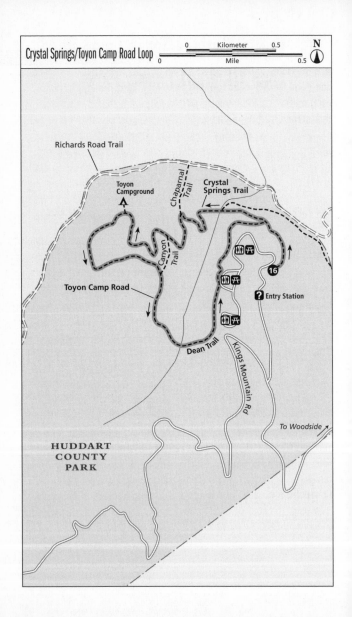

Crystal Springs/Toyon Camp Road Loop

Kilometer
0   0.5
Mile
0   0.5

N

Richards Road Trail

Toyon Campground

Chaparral Trail

Crystal Springs Trail

Canyon Trail

Toyon Camp Road

16

Entry Station

Dean Trail

Kings Mountain Rd

To Woodside

HUDDART COUNTY PARK

Finding the trailhead: The park is located at 1100 Kings Mountain Road. To reach the trailhead from Interstate 280 in Woodside, take the Highway 85/Woodside Road exit. Go right (west) on Woodside Road for 1.5 miles to Kings Mountain Road. Turn right (northwest) onto Kings Mountain Road and follow it for 2.1 miles to the park entrance on the right (east). Signs are posted along the route.

Follow the access road down to the entry kiosk. Park in the lot directly below the kiosk. The trailhead is in the northeast corner of the lot, opposite the ranger station. Parking is also available in lots next to the restrooms at the Zwierlein picnic area, 0.2 mile down the trail. *DeLorme: Northern California Atlas & Gazetteer:* Page 114 B3; GPS (upper parking lot trailhead): N37 26.432 / W122 17.493.

The Hike

Redwoods dominate the landscape of the Crystal Springs Trail through Huddart County Park. The sequoias overwhelm all other trees that attempt to grow within the boundaries of their groves, leaving room only for moss, ferns, and the occasional toyon or huckleberry. Their fragrant discarded needles form a thick, soft padding on the trail bed.

Oak woodlands creep in between the redwood groves— a more diverse community that includes various oaks, madrone, manzanita, and a wealth of wildflowers in spring.

Beginning opposite the ranger station, the trail descends to the Zweirlein trailhead, where it picks up the Crystal Springs Trail. Winding down through stands of redwoods, the path drops around two switchbacks into the McGarvey Gulch Creek drainage. A bridge facilitates the creek crossing in the rainy months. Regardless of the season, the hollow is thick with redwoods and rings with birdcalls.

Cross the bridge and begin the long, moderate climb out of the hollow and onto the slopes above. Switchbacks and sweeping traverses facilitate the ascent, leading through straight stands of redwood and leaning groves of oak and madrone. Pass intersections with the Chaparral Trail and the Canyon Trail (which offers a cutoff option) as you climb. The switchbacks between the Canyon Trail and the junction with the Richards Road Trail at the 2.0-mile mark total half a dozen. An access trail to the Toyon group camp lies 0.1 mile and a switchback above; the camp road, where the descent begins, is a redwood grove away.

Once on the Toyon Camp Road you travel on broken asphalt. Patches of sunlight, like the patches of pavement, quilt the descent. There is little traffic on the road; you may see an occasional vehicle, but chances are good that you and your fellow hikers will have the road to yourselves.

Pass the other end of the Canyon Trail as you drop to the Dean Trail at 3.2 miles. The Dean Trail, a dirt singletrack, leads left (east) around the Madrone and Werder picnic areas to the first intersection passed on the Crystal Springs Trail. Retrace your route from here to the trailhead.

Miles and Directions

0.0 Start in the upper lot at the trailhead across from the ranger station.

0.2 Descend from the parking area to the Zweirlein trailhead, passing more parking, sand volleyball courts, and the Bay Tree Trail junction. At the Crystal Spring trailhead adjacent to the restrooms, go left (north); the trail sign indicates that this leads to the Dean Trail intersection and the Phleger Estate.

0.4 Cross a culvert and pass two social trails on the left that climb to the picnic area above. Stay straight on the Crystal Springs Trail.

0.5 Pass the Dean Trail, which takes off to the left (west). This is part of the return route. Stay straight (right/north) on the Crystal Springs Trail, headed toward the Toyon camp and the Phleger Estate.

0.8 Arrive at the trail junction at McGarvey Creek. Go left (north) over the bridge to continue on the Crystal Springs Trail. The trail to the right leads down to the Phleger Estate.

1.0 Round a switchback and cross a seasonal stream.

1.1 Another switchback and traverse leads to the Chaparral Trail intersection. Stay left (southwest) on the Crystal Springs Trail.

1.4 Yet another switchback and traverse deposits you at the Canyon Trail junction. Stay straight (right/northwest) on the Crystal Springs Trail.

2.0 Switchbacks lead up to the intersection with the Richards Road Trail. Stay left (south) on the Crystal Springs Trail.

2.1 Arrive at an access trail for the Toyon camp; stay left (southeast) on the Crystal Springs Trail.

2.3 Pass a gate in a redwood grove and arrive at the Toyon Camp Road. Turn left (southeast), heading blessedly downhill under a canopy of oak and redwood toward the Dean Trail and the ranger station. The Crystal Springs Trail continues straight across the road.

2.8 Pass the Canyon Trail intersection at 2.8 miles on the left. Stay straight (right/southeast) on the Toyon Camp Road.

3.2 Turn left (east) off the camp road onto the Dean Trail, which skirts the Madrone and Werder picnic areas.

3.5 Arrive back at the Crystal Springs Trail. Turn right (south) onto the Crystal Springs Trail, and retrace your steps past the Zweirlein picnic area.

3.8 Reach the end of the loop at the parking lot.

Options: Huddart County Park is part of a cluster of contiguous open spaces on the slopes of the Santa Cruz Mountains above Woodside. The Phleger Estate, Teague Hill (with limited public access), and Purisima Redwoods Open Space Preserve adjoin the park and offer more opportunities to explore redwood country.

17 Salamander Flat Loop (Wunderlich County Park)

An easy climb through redwood glens and stands of euca-lyptus leads to Salamander Pond, a reservoir for the Folger Estate and the stomping grounds of the adorable rough-skinned newt.

Distance: 2.6-mile loop

Approximate hiking time: 1.5 hours

Difficulty: Moderate due to the length and the elevation change

Trail surface: Dirt singletrack, wide dirt trails

Best season: Year-round. This is a good choice on a hot summer day as it is mostly shady.

Other trail users: Equestrians, trail runners

Canine compatibility: Dogs not permitted

Fees and permits: No fees or permits required

Schedule: The park opens at 8:00 a.m. and closes at various times depending on the season. From April to August the park is open until 8:00 p.m. From November through February

gates close at 5:00 p.m.

Maps: USGS: Woodside; Wun-derlich County Park map and brochure available at the trail-head and online at www.eparks .net

Trail contacts: San Mateo County Department of Parks, 455 County Center Fourth Floor, Redwood City 94063-1646; (650) 363-4020; www.eparks .net; Wunderlich County Park direct line: (650) 851-1210

Special considerations: The park is home to a variety of wild-life, including potentially danger-ous rattlesnakes and mountain lions. Encounters are not com-mon, but hikers should know how to deal with either animal should their paths cross.

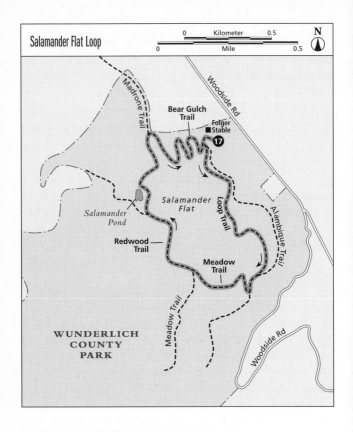

Salamander Flat Loop

Kilometer
Mile

N

Madrone Trail

Woodside Rd

Bear Gulch Trail

Folger Stable

17

Salamander Flat

Salamander Pond

Loop Trail

Redwood Trail

Alambique Trail

Meadow Trail

Meadow Trail

WUNDERLICH COUNTY PARK

Woodside Rd

Finding the trailhead: From Interstate 280 take the Sand Hill Road exit. Head west on Sand Hill Road for 2.1 miles to Portola Road. Turn right (north) onto Portola Road, which becomes Woodside Road, and drive 1.1 mile to the park entrance on the left (west) at 4040 Woodside Road. The trailhead is at the informational billboard (with trail maps) on the south side of the dirt parking area. *DeLorme: Northern California Atlas & Gazetteer:* Page 114 B3. GPS: N37 24.668 / W122 15.663.

The Hike

Bygone moguls of San Francisco have left remnants of their estates scattered about the Bay Area. Barons of railroads, sugar, coffee, and banking often held vast tracts of former Spanish ranchos in the countryside surrounding the fog and bustle of the city. Though most likely not their intent, the moguls preserved woodlands and grasslands in private ownership with minimal, albeit extravagant, development. Mansions, waterworks, stables, bathhouses, pleasure palaces—sometimes all of the above—were sprinkled on sprawling estates from Sonoma County to Woodside and beyond.

Some of these holdings have been passed along as gifts to cities and counties, which have in turn transformed them into parklands. Wunderlich County Park preserves a portion of the former estate of coffee magnate James Folger II, which sprawled along the foothills of the Santa Cruz Mountains west of Woodside. The park is home to the spectacular Folger Stable, an enormous, magnificent building—called a "horse palace" in a park brochure—that is on the National Register of Historic Places.

Under renovation beginning in late 2008, this rambling structure is a functioning stable, and it's not uncommon to encounter horses boarded there (and their riders, of course) on the trails that wind through the park's redwood groves and eucalyptus stands. Other Folger estate remnants, which date back to what park literature calls the Great Estates period at the turn of the twentieth century, include a carriage house, the stone walls that line trails and roads in the park, a blacksmith barn, and a dairy house down by the creek near the park's entrance.

While Folger's legacy is impressive, it would have little impact on the lives of Bay Area hikers if it weren't for the contribution made by the next property owner, Martin Wunderlich. In 1974 Wunderlich gave 942 acres to San Mateo County as a park, ensuring that generations to come would be able to enjoy both the man-made works preserved there and the natural beauty that surrounds them.

The loop to Salamander Flat follows wide trails that were once haul roads (the area was logged and the site of a sawmill in the mid-1800s), farm roads (the property was planted with orchards and vineyards in the late 1800s), and carriage roads. The inclines and declines are never too steep, and the width allows hikers to walk side by side, making this a great hike for families and small groups of friends.

Salamander Flat is actually Salamander Pond, a former estate reservoir now fenced off and serving as habitat for rough-skinned newts. About the cutest creepy-crawly you'll ever see, the orange-bellied newts emerge in wet weather and meander across hillside and trail to the pool. They can at times be a plague on the trail: Once you spot one, you'll see them everywhere, causing any conscientious hiker to dance and leap along the path to avoid squishing them.

The route also swings in and out of stands of native redwoods trees with a vibrant understory of fern and toyon, patches of oak woodland (watch the poison oak!), and groves of nonnative eucalyptus. All impart their unique light and scent to the loop. All trails are well signed and maintained, making route-finding a breeze.

Miles and Directions

0.0 Start on the Bear Gulch Trail on the south side of the stable.

0.2 After climbing behind the stable, then through a redwood grove and around a switchback, arrive at the intersection of the service road and Loop Trail. Go left (southwest) on the Loop Trail—a broad, easy, gently ascending trail wide enough to allow hikers to walk side by side and for equestrians to pass comfortably.

0.5 Curve through another redwood grove in a gully. The trail passes through alternating eucalyptus and redwood glades, with views opening occasionally over the treetops to the hills on the other side of the San Andreas Fault rift valley and the bay beyond.

1.0 Meet the Alambique Trail, which has been visible below the Loop Trail for the last 0.1 mile or so. Stay straight (right/southwest) on the Alambique Trail.

1.1 At the next trail intersection, go right (northwest) on the Meadow Trail toward Salamander Flat. The trail is well graded and wide—a phalanx of hikers could march up through the eucalyptus four abreast.

1.3 Reach the intersection with the Redwood Trail. Turn right (north) on the Redwood Trail, immediately entering a grove of the stately trees for which the trail is named. Swing through several gullies as you continue, one with a stair-step cascade that runs in the rainy season and is stone dry in late summer. A ramshackle pipe traces the latter portion of this trail section.

1.5 Arrive at the junction of the Redwood and Madrone Trails. Turn right (downhill and north) on the Madrone Trail. Salamander Flat and its brilliantly green algae-covered pool are about 75 yards down the Madrone Trail on the left (north). An interpretive sign describes the newts that hang out here in winter.

2.1 At the intersection of the Bear Gulch and Madrone Trails, make a sharp right (south) turn onto the Bear Gulch Trail.

2.4 Descend a series of switchbacks through the woods back to the service road/Loop Trail intersection passed earlier in the hike. A visit in late summer, when the poison oak has turned a glowing red, demonstrates how versatile the plant is, growing in vines up the oaks and in hedges along the trail.

2.6 Retrace your steps along the Bear Gulch Trail back to the Folger Stable and trailhead.

Options: After your hike, take fifteen minutes to tour the Folger estate buildings, including the stable, carriage house, and the stone walls and staircase that lead down to the parking lot.

If you want to extend your exploration of the park, you can create longer loops by continuing on any of the trails that make up part of this loop—Alambique (to Alambique Flat and beyond), Meadow (to the Meadows), and Redwood (to Redwood Flat).

18 Mount Ellen Summit Trail (San Mateo Memorial County Park)

There's one in every guidebook—the hike that one climbs simply for climbing's sake, testing lungs and legs both on the uphill run and the downhill. The Mount Ellen Trail is a lovely physical-fitness exam that can be followed by a cool-down in nearby Pescadero Creek and a night spent in the park's wooded campground.

Distance: 1.6-mile loop

Approximate hiking time: 1 hour

Difficulty: More challenging due to the uninterrupted ascent and descent

Trail surface: Dirt singletrack

Best season: Year-round

Other trail users: None

Canine compatibility: No dogs permitted

Fees and permits: $5 per car

Schedule: The park opens daily at 8:00 a.m. and closes at or before sunset, depending on the season. April through Labor Day, the park remains open until 8:00 p.m. November through February, the park closes at 5:00 p.m.

Maps: USGS: La Honda; San Mateo County Memorial Park brochure and map

Trail contact: San Mateo County Department of Parks, 455 County Center, Fourth Floor, Redwood City 94063-1646; (650) 363-4020; www.eparks.net; Memorial Visitor Center direct line: (650) 879-0212

Special considerations: This one's for hardy day hikers and should only be attempted by folks in good physical condition. Taken slowly and carefully, this trail is well within the reach of any able-bodied hiker, regardless of age.

Rattlesnakes can be found on Mount Ellen, so proceed with caution in the warm months of spring, summer, and fall.

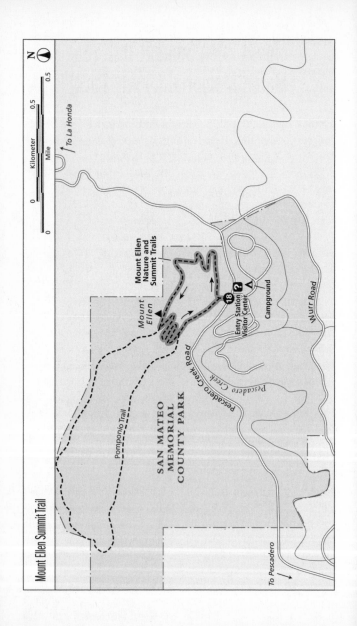

Mount Ellen Summit Trail

N

Mount Ellen Nature and Summit Trails

Mount Ellen

Pomponio Trail

SAN MATEO MEMORIAL COUNTY PARK

Pescadero Creek Road

Pescadero Creek

Entry Station Visitor Center

18

Campground

Wurr Road

To La Honda

To Pescadero

Kilometer
Mile

0   0.5

0   0.5

Additional information: Be sure to borrow a copy of the nature trail guide from the ranger at the entry kiosk. An alphabet's worth of sites are documented in the guide, marked by signposts at the beginning and end of the Mount Ellen Summit Trail.

Finding the trailhead: To reach the trailhead from the Cabrillo Highway south of Half Moon Bay, turn left (east) onto Pescadero Creek Road and travel 9.4 miles to the park entrance on the right (south). From La Honda, on Highway 35 south of San Francisco and west of Woodside, travel 6 miles west on Pescadero Creek Road to the park entrance. *DeLorme: Northern California Atlas & Gazetteer:* Page 114 B3. GPS: N37 16.584 / W122 17.490.

The Hike

Reaching the top of any peak is exhilarating, and Mount Ellen, though only 680 feet above sea level, is no exception. But it's not the views and altitude that make this a great day hike. It's the fact that you'll have climbed a dozen switchbacks to attain the summit—and have burned more than enough calories to validate a gooey s'more at camp in the evening.

The route has the added benefit of beginning and ending on a nature trail. Borrow a guide at the park's entry kiosk, and read all about the environment through which you climb and descend so quickly. The breaks, particularly on the climb, will be welcome rests.

The trail winds up and down through stands of pencil-straight redwoods, most of them second-growth, as the mountains were raided for lumber around the turn of the twentieth century. The redwoods mingle with Douglas fir, and both of these timber resources shelter an understory thick with ferns, huckleberry, and poison oak. It almost goes without saying that the presence of the latter discourages cross-country travel. The hills also host patches of oak woodland; the bark of the tan oak also was harvested here and used to preserve animal hides. At breaks in the canopy, views open of the wooded slopes of neighboring peaks in the Santa Cruz Mountains.

The hike begins across Pescadero Creek Road from the park's entry (elevation 250 feet), where you'll pay your fee and park. This is also the trailhead for the Mount Ellen Nature Trail (1.0 mile) and the Pomponio Trail (3.5 miles). Enter the woods and encounter the first switchback almost immediately, climbing to another intersection with the nature trail. By the time you round the second switchback, you'll have passed nature trail posts A through F and will be quickly gaining altitude.

The age of some of the trees in the forest is evident as you climb. A huge log that fell across the trail has been split, forming head-high walls on either side. Farther along, the thick gnarled roots of a fir form stair steps in the trail.

At the 0.5-mile mark the nature trail diverges from the summit trail, offering an easy out for those not up to the challenge. To continue to the top, switchback up and right (east) on the summit trail, then switchback again, and again.

But don't despair. The switchbacks are separated by long, gradually ascending traverses, where openings in the canopy afford views across the Pescadero Creek canyon. One of those long traverses swings to the east face of the mountain through a cluster of redwoods, then back to the south face, where bracken ferns raise broad fans toward the filtered sun. The canopy thins as you approach the summit; a pair of switchbacks deposits you on the ridgetop, where you can glimpse views in all directions. The summit, marked by a trail sign, is little more than a small, flat clearing on the wooded ridge, with trees rising on all sides.

At least sixteen switchbacks drop down the west ridge of the mountain, separated in some instances by long stretches of woodland rambling and at other times coming one on top of the next. Two intersections with the Pomponio Trail, which leads into the western heights of the park, are passed on the downhill run, along with a rattlesnake warning sign. Hook up with the nature trail, passing markers U through Z before arriving back at the first trail junction and the trailhead.

Miles and Directions

0.0 Start at the trailhead across Pescadero Creek Road from the park's entry kiosk.

0.1 Stay right (east) on the Mount Ellen Nature Trail.

0.5 The nature trail splits off the summit trail to the left (west). Stay right (east) on the switchbacking summit trail.

1.0 Climb switchbacks and traverses to the marked Mount Ellen summit. The descent begins.

1.2 Pass an intersection with the Pomponio Trail, continuing left (east) and down on the Mount Ellen Summit Trail.

1.4 Arrive at the junction with the Mount Ellen Nature Trail. Stay left (east) on the combined nature and summit trail, descending toward the ranger station.

1.5 Pass a second intersection with the Pomponio Trail and again stay left (east), continuing down on the summit/ nature trail.

1.6 Enjoy the shade of a glorious stand of redwoods on the final stretch, which drops past the last few nature trail markers and the first trail junction before arriving back at the trail-head.

Other: This park offers premium camping facilities, a summertime water hole, and fine short trails along Pescadero Creek. If you're not up for the Mount Ellen ascent, try the short loop along the Creek and Homestead Trails.

The interpretive center, located near the park's entry, is open daily from May to September. Naturalists offer programs at the park's amphitheater in the summer months.

19 Sequoia-Audubon Trail (Pescadero Marsh Natural Preserve)

Brambles and birdcalls engulf hikers in the lush marshlands just inland from Pescadero State Beach. From the incessant surf to the quiet hillside at trail's end, you'll be accompanied by critters underfoot and critters overhead, some of them rare and endangered.

Distance: 2.3 miles out and back

Approximate hiking time: 1.5 hours

Difficulty: Easy

Trail surface: Sand and dirt singletrack

Best season: Year-round. Your best bet for sunshine and warmth is in September and October. The best bird watching is in spring and late autumn.

Other trail users: Trail runners

Canine compatibility: No dogs permitted

Fees and permits: Parking fees are levied at the north beach parking lot, but not at the south beach lot or the middle lot, which is closest to the trailhead. The downside to this fee-free and unstaffed parking lot: Vehicles

have been vandalized on occasion. Do not leave valuables in your car.

Schedule: Beach day-use areas, including the trail, open 8:00 a.m. to sunset daily

Maps: USGS: San Gregorio; Pescadero Marsh Natural Preserve Sequoia-Audubon Trail map on the California State Parks Web site at www.parks.ca.gov

Trail contact: California State Parks, Department of Parks and Recreation, 1416 Ninth Street, Sacramento 95814 (mailing address: P.O. Box 942896, Sacramento 94296); (650) 879-2170; www.parks.ca.gov

Special considerations: Winter storms or dense fog can soak and chill hikers at any time of year. Dress in layers and be prepared for changeable weather.

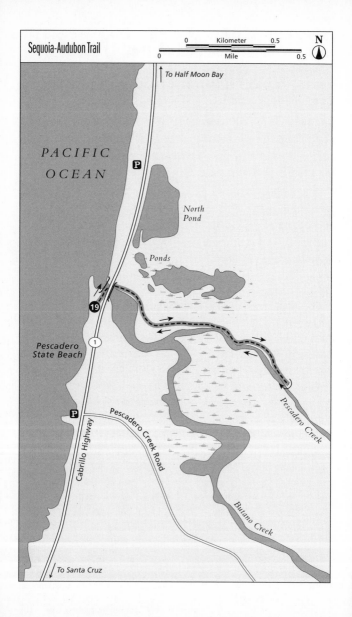

Sequoia-Audubon Trail

0   Kilometer   0.5
0   Mile   0.5

N

To Half Moon Bay

PACIFIC
OCEAN

North
Pond

Ponds

19

Pescadero
State Beach

1

Pescadero Creek Road

Cabrillo Highway

Pescadero Creek

Butano Creek

To Santa Cruz

Finding the trailhead: Pescadero State Beach is located about 14 miles south of Half Moon Bay on the Cabrillo Highway (Highway 1). Park in the middle Pescadero Beach parking area, just over the bridge that spans Butano Creek. *DeLorme: Northern California Atlas & Gazetteer:* Page 114 B2. GPS (parking lot): N37 15.926 / W122 24.725.

The Hike

Pescadero Marsh is no destination for the hiker in a hurry. The disorganized surf on Pescadero State Beach, depending on how raucous its mood, may inspire a quick step at the trailhead, but once you mount the levee that borders Butano Creek and the still waters of the wetland, your pace will slow. Treading lightly and quietly brings forth the songbirds that flit through the brush, the shorebirds that harvest the waterways, and the rare reptiles that call the 600-acre marsh home.

The trail is lined with interpretive signs that describe the flora and fauna of the marsh—200 species of plants can be found in the preserve, and 230 species of birds either live in or visit the marsh annually. The rich, waterlogged habitat supports the endangered red-legged frog and San Francisco garter snake. Depending on the season, plant life on the dunes near the trail's beginning includes bush lupine, clover, ice plant, twinberry, Indian paintbrush, wild mustard, and yarrow. Farther upstream, vegetation more typical of riparian zones and oak woodlands takes over, pushing with vigor against the trail's edge.

Begin by taking the stairs from the south end of the parking lot. Follow the pedestrian walkway along the highway bridge and drop onto Pescadero State Beach. The marsh is on the east side of the highway, reached via a sandy slog under the bridge and over the litter of driftwood. Several social trails wind through the dunes on the east side of the highway, but the Sequoia–Audubon route is well marked.

Wander for about 0.5 mile through the dunes before climbing onto the levee, where an interpretive sign warns of the dangers posed by a pair of plants native to the marsh—poison oak and stinging nettle. Taking care to stay on the path will ensure you don't have a close encounter with one of these "untouchables." Keep an eye on the wall of eucalyptus bounding the marsh on the left (north); this is a blue heron rookery from March trough August.

The vegetation in this environment gradually grows taller and vaguely oppressive as you head inland. Pass an amazingly twisted old eucalyptus before the trail begins a gradual ascent through walls of greenery. Watch the dirt track for sign of the rare San Francisco garter snake (or the more common black variety); you may also hear the crash of larger animals hidden behind the thick hedge.

Break free of the bramble bower at the base of the hillside near trail's end, and mount two quick switchbacks to a bench and a weathered, virtually unreadable interpretive sign that appears to describe raptors and other birds of the marsh. The spectacular vista sweeps down across the marsh to the beach and the ocean beyond. When you've absorbed as much of the view as you desire, retrace your steps to the trailhead.

Miles and Directions

0.0   Start at the middle Pescadero State Beach parking lot, with a restroom and trash container. Drop to the side of the Cabrillo Highway via a short staircase and turn left (north).

0.2   Follow the highway bridge and drop left (west) onto Pescadero State Beach at the mouth of Butano Creek. An interpretive panel and trail sign mark the trailhead proper (GPS:

N37 16.058 / W122 24.660). Walk south down the beach toward the creek, then turn left (east) and pass under the bridge.

0.4 Reach the Sequoia-Audubon Trail sign. Follow the obvious sandy path up into the dunes, passing an informational sign about steelhead trout. At the trail fork stay right (east) on the Sequoia-Audubon Trail.

0.6 After passing a social trail that leads right (south) to the beach along the creek, reach the junction with the North Pond Trail. Stay right (east) on the Sequoia-Audubon Trail, which climbs onto the raised bank along Butano Creek.

0.7 Pass a levee gate and an interpretive sign that describes seasonal changes in the marsh.

0.8 A cool, twisted eucalyptus unfurls along the south side of the trail, and an interpretive sign describes the blue heron rookery on the north side of the marsh.

0.9 One sign describes the red-legged frog, followed shortly by a second sign describing the San Francisco garter snake, which eats the frogs.

1.1 The trailside brambles grow taller and thicker as you pass a sign describing the dusky-footed wood rat (or pack rat). It's pretty obvious where the rodent gets the sticks it needs to build its nest.

1.2 Two switchbacks lead up a scrubby hillside to the trail's end at a viewing bench. Return as you came.

1.7 Arrive back at the North Pond trail intersection. Add a little variety to the end of the hike by turning right (north) onto the North Pond Trail and crossing a boardwalk with a viewing bench before climbing back onto the levee.

1.9 At the intersection with the Sequoia-Audubon Trail, go left (south) on the Sequoia-Audubon Trail, heading back toward Butano Creek. From here, retrace your steps to the trailhead.

2.3 Climb back to the Cabrillo Highway, head south across the highway bridge, and arrive back at the parking area.

Appendix: The Art of Hiking

When standing nose to nose with a mountain lion, you're probably not too concerned with the issue of ethical behavior in the wild. No doubt you're just terrified. But let's be honest. How often are you nose to nose with a mountain lion? For most of us, a hike into the "wild" means loading up the SUV with expensive gear and driving to a toileted trailhead. Sure, you can mourn how civilized we've become—how GPS units have replaced natural instinct and Gore-Tex, true-grit—but the silly gadgets of civilization aside, we have plenty of reason to take pride in how we've matured. With survival now on the back burner, we've begun to reason—and it's about time—that we have a responsibility to protect, no longer just conquer, our wild places: that they, not we, are at risk. So please, do what you can. The following section will help you understand better what it means to "do what you can" while still making the most of your hiking experience. Anyone can take a hike, but hiking safely and well is an art requiring preparation and proper equipment.

Trail Etiquette

Keep your dog under control. You can buy a flexi-lead that allows your dog to go exploring along the trail, while allowing you the ability to reel him in should another hiker approach or should he decide to chase a rabbit. Always obey leash laws and be sure to bury your dog's waste or pack it in resealable plastic bags.

Respect other trail users. Often you're not the only one on the trail. With the rise in popularity of multiuse trails, you'll have to learn a new kind of respect, beyond the nod and "hello" approach you may be used to. First investigate whether you're on a multiuse trail, and assume the appropriate precautions. When you encounter motorized vehicles (ATVs, motorcycles, and 4WDs), be alert. Though they should always yield to the hiker, often they're going too fast or are too lost in the buzz of their engine to react to your presence. If you hear activity ahead, step off the trail just to be safe. Note that you're not likely to hear a mountain biker coming, so be prepared and know ahead of time whether you share the trail with them. Cyclists should always yield to hikers, but that's little comfort to the hiker. Be aware. When you approach horses or pack animals on the trail, always step quietly off the trail, preferably on the downhill side, and let them pass. If you're wearing a large backpack, it's often a good idea to sit down. To some animals, a hiker wearing a large backpack might appear threatening. Many national forests allow domesticated grazing, usually for sheep and cattle. Make sure your dog doesn't harass these animals, and respect ranchers' rights while you're enjoying yours.

Be Prepared

Getting into shape. Unless you want to be sore—and possibly have to shorten your trip or vacation—be sure to get in shape before your hike, even if you're planning a short one. Start with a fifteen-minute walk during your lunch hour or after work and gradually increase your walking time to an hour. You should also increase your elevation gain. Walking briskly up hills really strengthens your leg muscles and gets your heart rate up. If you work in a storied office building, take the stairs instead of the elevator. If you prefer going to a gym, walk the treadmill or use a stair machine. You can further increase your strength and endurance by walking with a loaded backpack. Stationary exercises you might consider are squats, leg lifts, sit-ups, and push-ups. Other good ways to get in shape include biking, running, aerobics, and, of course, short hikes. Stretching before and after a hike keeps muscles flexible and helps avoid injuries.

Water. Even in frigid conditions, you need at least two quarts of water a day to function efficiently. Add heat and taxing terrain and you can bump that figure up to one gallon. That's simply a base to work from—your metabolism and your level of conditioning can raise or lower that amount. Unless you know your level, assume that you need one gallon of water a day.

Trip Planning. Planning your hiking adventure begins with letting a friend or relative know your trip itinerary so they can call for help if you don't return at your scheduled time. Your next task is to make sure you are outfitted to experience the risks and rewards of the trail. This section suggests gear and clothing you may want to take with you to get the most out of your day hike.

- camera/film
- compass/GPS unit
- pedometer
- daypack
- first-aid kit
- food
- guidebook
- headlamp/flashlight with extra batteries and bulbs
- hat
- insect repellent

- knife/multipurpose tool
- map
- matches in waterproof container and fire starter
- fleece jacket
- rain gear
- space blanket
- sunglasses
- sunscreen
- swimsuit
- watch
- water
- water bottles/water hydration system

Hiking with Children

Hiking with children isn't a matter of how many miles you can cover or how much elevation gain you make in a day; it's about seeing and experiencing nature through their eyes.

Kids like to explore and have fun. They like to stop and point out bugs and plants, look under rocks, jump in puddles, and throw sticks. If you're taking a toddler or young child on a hike, start with a trail that you're familiar with. Trails that have interesting things for kids, like piles of leaves to play in or a small stream to wade through during the summer, will make the hike much more enjoyable for them and will keep them from getting bored.

You can keep your child's attention if you have a strategy before starting on the trail. Using games is not only an effective way to keep a child's attention, it's also a great way to teach him or her about nature. Play hide and seek, where your child is the mouse and you are the hawk. Quiz children on the names of plants and animals. If your children are old enough, let them carry their own daypack filled with snacks and water. So that you are sure to go at their pace and not yours, let them lead the way. Playing follow the leader works particularly well when you have a group of children. Have each child take a turn at being the leader.

With children, a lot of clothing is key. The only thing predictable about weather is that it will change. Always bring extra clothing for children, regardless of the season. In the winter you should consider wool socks and warm layers such as long underwear, a fleece jacket and hat, wool mittens, and good rain gear for your child. Good footwear is also important. A sturdy pair of high top tennis shoes or lightweight hiking boots are the best bet for little ones. If you're hiking in the summer near a lake or stream, bring along a pair of old sneakers that your child can put on when he wants to go exploring in the water. Remember when you're near any type of water, watch your child at all times. Also, keep a close eye on teething toddlers who may decide a rock or leaf of poison oak is an interesting item to put in their mouth.

From spring through fall you'll want your kids to wear a wide-brimmed hat to keep their face, head, and ears protected from the hot sun. Also, make sure your children wear sunscreen at all times. Choose a brand without Paba—children have sensitive skin and may have an allergic reaction to sunscreen that contains Paba. If you are hiking with a child younger than six months, don't use sunscreen or insect repellent. Instead, be sure that their head, face, neck, and ears are protected from the sun with a wide-brimmed hat, and that all other skin exposed to the sun is protected with the appropriate clothing.

Remember that food is fun. Kids like snacks so it's important to bring a lot of munchies for the trail. Stopping often for snack breaks is a fun way to keep the trail interesting. Raisins, apples, granola bars, crackers and cheese, cereal, and trail mix all make great snacks. If your child is old enough to carry her own backpack, fill it with treats before you leave. If your kids don't like drinking water, you can bring boxes of fruit juice.

About the Author

Tracy Salcedo-Chourré has written more than a dozen guidebooks to destination in Colorado and California, including *Hiking Lassen Volcanic National Park, Exploring California's Missions and Presidios, Exploring Point Reyes National Seashore and the Golden Gate National Recreation Area, Best Rail Trails California,* and *Best Easy Day Hikes* guides to Denver, Boulder, Aspen, and Lake Tahoe.

She is also an editor, teacher, and soccer mom—and still finds time to hike, cycle, swim, and ski.

Tracy lives with her husband, three sons, and small menagerie of pets in California's wine country.